D1028896

The Sick Book

QUESTIONS AND ANSWERS ABOUT HICCUPS AND MUMPS SNEEZES AND BUMPS AND OTHER THINGS THAT GO WRONG WITH US

written by Marie Winn

illustrated by Fred Brenner

diagrams by Honi Werner

Medical Consultant:

Dr. Kenneth McIntosh
Associate Professor of Pediatrics
University of Colorado Medical Center
Denver, Colorado

FOUR WINDS PRESS   NEW YORK

to my father

Library of Congress Cataloging in Publication Data

Winn, Marie
  The sick book.

  Summary: Simple questions and answers reveal what happens to the
body during many common illnesses and injuries such as bruises, broken
bones, allergies, colds, indigestion, and chicken pox.

  1. Medicine — Juvenile literature. [1. Medicine]
I. Brenner, Fred. II. Title.
R130.5.W56   616   75–34470
ISBN 0–590–07259–5

Published by Four Winds Press
A Division of Scholastic Magazines, Inc., New York, N.Y.
Text copyright © 1976 by Marie Winn
Illustrations copyright © 1976 by Fred Brenner
All Rights Reserved
Printed in the United States of America
Library of Congress Catalog Card Number: 75-34470
1 2 3 4 5   80 79 78 77 76

Contents

Introduction

Long ago people had some funny ideas about sickness. They thought that ghosts and goblins and evil spirits made people sick. And they believed that getting sick was a punishment for doing bad things or even thinking bad thoughts. They tried sending prayers and presents to the ghosts and goblins and evil spirits to keep sickness away. They tried being very, very good and only thinking good thoughts. But no matter what they did people still became sick. And being sick was very unpleasant.

Today we know that ghosts and goblins and spirits have nothing to do with sickness. We know that being bad or thinking bad thoughts cannot make anyone sick. But being sick is just as unpleasant today as it ever was. The things that happen to you when you're sick—runny noses, sore throats, stomachaches, earaches, coughs, and sneezes—these things are always annoying and make you very uncomfortable. And so people still think that being sick is something bad.

Well, here is something that may surprise you: MOST OF THE THINGS THAT HAPPEN TO YOU WHEN

YOU'RE SICK ARE GOOD FOR YOU! Those unpleasant things are actually your body's way of fighting trouble and keeping you healthy!

This book is about what happens to your body when you're sick. It is not about very special sicknesses that only happen to a few unlucky people. It is about colds and sore throats and stomachaches and other ordinary things that happen to almost everybody once in a while. It will explain how things work when you're sick. And maybe, when you understand how each of these unpleasant things works, it might make being sick a little less unpleasant. Even if it doesn't help you feel better, at least it will make being sick less frightening and much more interesting.

The Sick Book

PART ONE

1

Wait a Minute!
Before You Start. . .

When you are sick your body works in different ways than when you are healthy. The questions and answers in this book are about those *different* things your body does when you're sick.

But sometimes it is hard to understand how things work when you're sick if you don't know how your body works when you're healthy.

The last chapter of this is called HOW IT WORKS. It answers questions about different parts of your body and how they work when you're healthy. You can use this chapter to help you understand *The Sick Book* by using the little symbols that you'll find next to most of the questions and answers about sickness.

Each symbol stands for a different section of the HOW IT WORKS chapter:

 stands for The Cell on page 109.

 stands for Digestion on page 113.

stands for Blood and Circulation on page 117.

 stands for Breathing on page 123.

 stands for The Skin on page 126.

 stands for Bones on page 130.

 stands for Muscles on page 130

 stands for Nerves on page 135.

If you want more information, or if there's something you don't understand about any question or answer, look at the symbol or symbols next to it and then turn to the HOW IT WORKS section or sections that the symbols stand for.

For instance, next to the question *Why does a mosquito bite itch?* (page 82), you will find the symbol

Since the answer to that question talks about nerves, you will have a better idea of why a mosquito bite itches if you turn to the HOW IT WORKS section about nerves on page 135 and find out more about nerves and how they work.

2 Sickness: What's It All About?

What is sickness?

Sickness is the name for what happens to you when your body starts doing some things in a different way than it usually does. Coughing and sneezing are different from your usual way of breathing. A runny nose is different from the way your nose usually works. Throwing up is very different from the way your stomach usually works. These different things your body does when you are sick are called *symptoms* (sím-tums).

Why do you get sick and have all sorts of different symptoms?

When there is some trouble inside your body, your body doesn't stop running and wait for somebody to come and fix it. The body can actually *fix the trouble itself* when something goes wrong! But when the body has to work at fighting trouble and fixing things up, then it cannot work in its usual way. At those times the body has to work in special, different ways. You know the body is working differently because you feel sick. You have different symptoms that let you know that your body is fighting trouble. When the trouble is fixed, then your body goes back to its good old way of running. You feel fine again.

What kinds of trouble can happen to the body that keep it from working the usual way?

Your body is made up of an enormous number of tiny cells. These are alive. They do all the work that keeps your body running. If anything happens to hurt or kill these important cells or to stop these cells from doing their jobs, that means TROUBLE. Then the body has to get to work to protect its cells and get rid of the trouble.

What happens in your body when any cells are hurt or killed?

When cells are hurt or killed in your body, it reacts in a very special way. This special reaction is called *inflammation* (in-fluh-máy-shun). Inflammation is one of your body's most important ways of fighting trouble.

What happens when you have an inflammation reaction?

Four things always happen when your body fights trouble with inflammation: swelling, redness, heat and pain.

What causes the swelling in an inflammation reaction?

When cells are hurt in some way the walls of the blood tubes in the area begin to leak out more fluid than they usually do. This extra fluid leaked out of the blood tubes causes most of the swelling when you have an inflammation somewhere in your body. Also, when you have an injury, the blood tubes in the area stretch and grow a little bigger in order to send more blood to the area to help fight trouble. This also causes some of the swelling.

What causes the redness in an inflammation reaction?

The tiny blood tubes are fairly transparent (you can see through them). When they stretch in an inflammation, you can simply see more blood. This causes the redness.

What causes the extra heat in an inflammation reaction?

The extra blood that has rushed to the spot is bringing with it extra heat.

What causes the pain in an inflammation reaction?

The swelling and the blood tubes stretching out press against some pain nerves in the area. They send a message to the brain, and you feel pain.

How does the body know when to start an inflammation reaction?

When cells are injured they let out a special chemical called *histamine* (hís-tuh-mean). This chemical starts the inflammation reaction.

What good does an inflammation reaction do?

When you have an inflammation reaction, extra blood rushes to the spot and extra fluid leaks out of the blood tubes. This brings many extra white blood cells to the injured area, and white blood cells fight germs. The extra blood also brings with it more food for energy and more cells to repair the damage.

What can hurt or kill cells in your body?

Injuries, too much heat, or too much cold will hurt or kill cells. But *germs* are the main troublemakers for the cells of the body. Fighting germs is one of the body's biggest jobs. Most of the things that happen to you when you are sick have something to do with your body's fight against germs.

3

Germs: The Bad Guys (and Sometimes the Good Guys)

What are germs?

Germs are tiny plants or animals. They are everywhere around you — in the air, in water, in the ground, and in almost every part of your body. But germs are so small that you cannot see them without the help of a microscope (a special instrument that makes small things look bigger).

Are all germs bad for people?

Not at all. Only certain special germs make you sick if they get inside your body. Many germs are useful to people. Some germs help fertilize the soil to make food grow better. Some germs help make water clean for drinking. And some germs inside your body actually work to keep you healthy.

What can germs do inside your body that helps keep you healthy?

Different germs can help in different ways. Some germs make vitamins in your body that are important for your health. Some germs fight against other harmful germs and keep those germs from settling down and causing trouble. And some germs help your body digest food.

Why do some germs make you sick and others don't?

Some germs make their way into your intestines where digestion of food takes place. They can live and grow there without doing any harm to any of your body's cells. They can live on parts of food that your body wouldn't use anyhow—food that will end up as waste materials. Those same germs also help the body break down and digest some of the food that the body *can* use. These germs are helpful. They do not make people sick.

But some germs get into other parts of the body where there is no extra food for them to live on. Then they settle down and use the body's cells for food. The body has to fight to get rid of these germs. The result of this fight is YOU GET SICK.

What germs *do* make people sick?

Two important kinds of germs cause most of our sicknesses: *bacteria* and *viruses*.

What are bacteria?

Bacteria are tiny one-celled creatures. Although each bacterium is made up of only one cell, that one cell does all the work that the many cells of a human being do: it takes in food, it gives out wastes, and it can give birth to a new cell just like itself.

Are all bacteria the same?

No, there are many different bacteria. Different bacteria act differently when they get into the body. That is one reason why there are different sicknesses.

What are viruses?

Viruses are germs that are even smaller than bacteria. Most viruses are too small to be seen even under a regular microscope. Only a special microscope that can make things look over *fifty thousand times* bigger than they really are can be used to look at viruses. Viruses are neither plants nor animals. They are smaller than both. They cannot live on their own. They go inside living cells and use the work of the cells to keep themselves alive. Viruses can also force living cells to make new viruses. In this way many viruses end up destroying cells.

Are all viruses the same?

No. There are many kinds of viruses that cause many different sicknesses.

How do germs get inside your body?

You have a natural armor that you wear all the time to protect you from germs, but it is not the heavy armor knights used to wear long ago. Your armor is your skin! Your skin keeps germs from getting into your body. Germs can only get in through one of the natural openings like the mouth or the nose. And even those natural openings have weapons that guard against germs. But if you get a break in your armor, like a cut or a scratch, then germs can get into the body through the break.

What happens if germs get into the body through the mouth?

Most germs that find their way into your mouth are swallowed. They go down the food canal into your stomach. In your stomach are some very strong acids called digestive juices. These acids will kill most germs. Only a very few germs are strong enough to keep on living in the stomach without being killed by the digestive juices. If you happen to swallow one of *those* very strong germs then you will probably get sick. Those are the germs that cause diarrhea or food poisoning.

What happens if germs get into the body through the nose?

The nose leads to the lungs. If germs manage to get into the lungs they can cause a lot of trouble. But fortunately the nose has a way of keeping most germs out of the lungs. The nose is lined with special cells that make a special, sticky liquid called *mucus* (mew-cuss). When germs get inside the nose they are caught by the sticky mucus. They cannot get by to the lungs.

Do the nose and the mouth keep *all* germs out of the body?

The body's natural defenses in the nose and the mouth work better against bacteria than viruses. Viruses sometimes manage to cause trouble in spite of your protection in the nose and mouth. That's one reason why you get so many colds and virus infections, and not so many sicknesses caused by bacteria.

What happens to the germs caught in the mucus inside your nose?

There are little hairs growing all over the inside of your nose. They are too tiny to see or even feel, but they are there. Each hair is attached to a tiny muscle that can wave the hair back and forth. The tiny hairs in your nose are moving all the time, even though you cannot feel them. They act as brooms, sweeping the mucus out of your nose and down into your throat. Once the mucus with all the trapped germs (and dust and anything else that might get caught there) goes into the throat it is swallowed. The germs go into the stomach. There they are killed by the strong stomach acids.

How do the germs that get inside your body make you sick?

Germs don't have anything bad in mind when they settle down inside your body. They just want to live their quiet lives, eating and multiplying. Unfortunately, what they want to eat are the living cells of your body. And when they eat they have to give off wastes, just as you do and every other living creature does. These wastes are sometimes strong poisons that may hurt cells of your body.

Since you need your body's cells to do all the different jobs that keep your body healthy, your body cannot let germs settle down to live and eat. And so your body starts doing some special things to get rid of the germs. Those special things your body does cause the symptoms that you feel when you are sick. It is your own body working in different ways to get rid of germs that makes you feel sick, not the germs themselves.

What would happen if the body didn't fight the germs?

Germs have one bad habit that makes them so dangerous: they multiply. One germ splits into 2 germs, the 2 germs split into 4, the 4 become 8, then 16, then 32, then 64, then 128, and so on. Pretty soon one germ will have multiplied into hundreds and thousands and even millions of germs. If the body didn't somehow stop the germs, soon there would be too many of them. They would destroy too many of the body's cells. Then the body could not go on living.

Are germs the only thing that ever make you sick?

Most sicknesses with names, like measles, mumps, or the flu are caused by germs. Pimples and boils and even warts are caused by germs too. When you get a cut that becomes red and filled with pus, germs are at work there, too. These are called *infections*. But there are other things that cause sicknesses. Some people are sick because they are *allergic* to certain things. You can read about that in the chapter on Allergies. You can fall the wrong way and break a bone or hurt a muscle. You won't feel too well when that happens but that kind of sickness is not caused by germs. The chapter called Breaks and Sprains tells how broken bones and sprained muscles happen and how they can be fixed. Sunburn and frostbite and car sickness are a few other troubles that are not caused by germs. You will read about these things later in the book. But germs are the most common troublemakers. They are the cause of most sicknesses.

4 Let's Take Your Temperature

Why do you have to have your temperature taken?

When a machine stops working you can take it apart to find out what's wrong. But when you're not feeling well, it's a little hard to take you apart without making you feel considerably worse.

One of the ways to find out what's going on inside you without actually looking inside is to check and see if anything about your body is working differently from the way it usually works.

The usual temperature inside your body is around 98 degrees. When you have your temperature taken the thermometer can tell you if your inside temperature is any different than usual. If the thermometer shows that your inside temperature is even two degrees higher than usual that means that something is definitely wrong.

A higher temperature inside your body is called a *fever.*

What does a fever do for you?

A fever is one of your body's important ways of fighting trouble. When you have a fever the extra heat makes more blood travel quickly around the body. This blood brings with it more food for parts of your body that are fighting germs and need extra strength. Most important of all, the blood brings with it extra white blood cells. These special cells can kill the germs that are causing the trouble.

Why does your skin feel tight and funny when you have a fever?

When you are getting a fever your skin stops sweating for a while. Sweating is one of the body's ways of keeping the inside temperature from getting hotter than the normal temperature of 98 degrees, even when its hotter than that outside. Sweating cools the body down.

But when you stop sweating, your temperature will get higher. This is one of the ways your body makes a fever. When you stop sweating your skin feels hot and dry and very different from the way it usually feels. This is the reason you have that tight and funny feeling when you have a fever.

Why do you sometimes get the shivers and shakes when you have a fever?

Usually you shiver and shake only when its very cold. It seems strange to get the shivers when you're hot with a fever. But the shivering you do when you have a fever is doing the same job for you that it does on a freezing day. Here's how it works:

On a cold day your body needs extra heat to keep the inside temperature from going lower than the usual 98 degrees. And so your brain sends a signal to many muscles inside your body: BEGIN TO SHIVER AND SHAKE! When muscles move very quickly they make heat. This heat warms you up inside and keeps your inside temperature from getting too low.

The shivering you do when you have a fever also makes heat. This time, though, the body needs to make the temperature *higher* than 98 degrees, in order to fight an infection. The brain sends a signal and your muscles begin to shiver and shake again—this time to raise your body temperature to a fever. You don't shiver *because* you have a fever; you have a fever *because* you are shivering.

How does your body know when to raise the temperature and give you a fever?

Some of the germs that have settled down in your body when you are sick give off wastes. These wastes get into your blood. When the blood with the germ wastes reaches the brain on its way around the body it goes through a special place that controls the temperature. Here the germ wastes leave a special message: LOOK OUT! GERMS AT WORK SOMEWHERE! The brain then sends a message back to different parts of the body: START WORKING DIFFERENTLY! The sweat glands stop sweating. Little muscles start shivering and shaking. Soon you have a fever.

What makes the temperature go down when you stop having a fever?

You can often tell that the worst part of a sickness is over when you suddenly break out into a sweat. This is a sign that your body doesn't need the fever to fight the germs any more. The sweating cools the body off and brings down the temperature. Now your brain has received the message: ALL CLEAR! DANGER FROM GERMS IS OVER! Soon everything starts working the same old way again.

If a fever helps your body fight sickness, why do you take aspirin to bring a fever down?

A fever can be helpful, but a very high fever can be dangerous, too. The high heat may be harmful to some of your body's cells, especially in the brain. Therefore it is important to try to bring down a high fever and aspirin is one of the best ways to bring a fever down. Even when a fever is not dangerous it usually makes you feel very uncomfortable. Taking an aspirin can help you feel better.

How does aspirin work to bring a fever down?

Scientists and doctors today can do many marvelous things and know a great deal about how the body works. They can transplant a heart from one person to another. They can cure diseases that were once thought incurable. But they still do not really understand how aspirin works! All they know is that it does!

Can you have a "reverse fever" and have too low a temperature?

Unless you are actually freezing to death you cannot have too low a temperature. But your temperature *does* change throughout the day and sometimes it is quite normal to have a temperature a little below 98 degrees, especially right after an infection.

Can anything else besides an infection give you a fever?

If you take your temperature right after running around and playing hard you may seem to have a fever.

That is because all your muscles' hard work has made a lot of heat. But your temperature will go down to normal as soon as you rest for a few moments. That is not a real fever.

A real fever cannot be caused by playing very hard. A fever is almost always caused by an infection of some kind in your body. Your temperature will stay high with a fever even when you a resting. To find out if you have a fever it is important not to take your temperature right after running around and playing. Take your temperature after resting for a while. If you have a fever you will be sure that it is a fever, and not just the extra heat your muscles have made because of hard exercise.

5

Eek! I'm Bleeding!
(Cuts, Scratches, Bruises, and Nosebleeds)

When you get a cut on your skin, why doesn't all the blood run out?

If your body were filled with plain water instead of blood, then it *would* all run out as soon as you got the smallest cut. But blood is very different from plain water. There is a special substance in your blood that goes to work when you get a cut. It makes the blood around the cut get thicker and thicker. Pretty soon the blood is so thick that it forms a solid sort of plug at the place where you cut yourself. This plug is called a *clot.* The clot acts like a cork. It keeps more blood from running out.

Why does the special substance in your blood make clots only when you get a cut?

It would be terrible if the special clotting substance in your blood worked all the time. Your blood would get thicker and thicker. Pretty soon it wouldn't be able to go around and around your body. Luckily, most of the time that special clotting substance just sits in the blood doing nothing. But when you get a cut, some cells are injured. These cells let out another special substance. Let's call it the *injury substance*. Only when the clotting substance gets together with the injury substance can it begin to work to make a clot. That's why your blood makes a clot only when you get a cut or injury somewhere in your body.

How long does it take for blood to form a clot?

Not very long. In a test tube blood takes from four to eight minutes to change from a thin liquid to a thick mass that will not pour out of the test tube at all.

What is that thick, yellowish stuff that sometimes shows up in a cut while it's healing?

That stuff is pus. Pus in a cut is a sign that the cut is infected with germs and that your body is fighting the infection.

What is pus?

One of the weapons your body uses in its fight against germs is the white blood cell. There are millions of white blood cells floating around in your blood all the time. When germs are causing trouble somewhere in the body, your body sends out its special troops—the white blood cells. The white blood cells rush to the spot where the germs have settled and attack the germs by surrounding them and actually swallowing and killing them. But in the course of the fight between germs and white blood cells some of the white blood cells get killed, too. When the battle is over there is usually quite a mess of dead germs and white blood cells on the battlefield. The name of this messy leftover is *pus*. Pus always looks thick and yellowish.

Why does the skin around a cut get all red and puffy even after it has stopped bleeding?

The swelling is a sign of your body's main defense system—inflammation. An extra supply of blood with germ-killing white blood cells has rushed to the spot to fight the germs. This causes the swelling and redness.

Why does the skin around an infected cut feel hotter than the skin on other parts of the body?

The temperature of the skin has a lot to do with how fast and how much blood is moving under the skin. The faster the blood moves, the higher the temperature of the skin. When you get a cut, more blood comes rushing to the spot at a faster speed than it usually takes in the body. This quick and increased flow of blood makes the temperature go up in the area where you have your cut.

When you cut yourself and the skin is broken, how does the skin heal again?

Your body produces a special repair cell. These repair cells are brought by the blood to the place where you have a cut. The repair cells help close the wound so that no more germs can get into the body.

Why do some cuts heal completely and others leave scars?

When you get a thin, straight, small cut, the repair cells bind the sides of the cut together. The cells at the sides of the cut simply grow together and close up the break in the skin. Then the skin looks the same as before the cut. The repair cells only help keep the sides of the cut together while it is healing. When the cut is healed they are cleared away by the blood.

But when you get a large, jagged cut the repair cells cannot pull the edges together completely. The cut is too uneven. Instead, they have to form a sort of bridge over the gap between the sides of the cut. Then they stay there. These repair cells, however, are a different kind of cell from your regular skin cells. And so the bridge they form looks different than the skin around it. The bridge formed by the repair cells to heal a wound is called scar tissue. It looks tougher and whiter than regular skin.

Why do some cuts need stitches?

Most cuts would probably heal without stitches. But when a cut is big and jagged you would probably end up with a lot of ugly scar tissue that formed while the cut was healing.

When the doctor stitches up a cut, the stitches bring the sides of the cut together. Then the cells of the sides of the cut can simply grow together again without needing a bridge of repair cells between them. In this way you end up with hardly any scar, or no scar at all, even when you get a large, jagged cut.

Why does it hurt when you cut yourself?

The pain that you feel when you get a cut or injury is actually one of your body's most important warnings. You have a system of pain nerves all through your body. When you hurt yourself those pain nerves signal very quickly: STOP WHAT YOU'RE DOING! YOU'RE DOING SOMETHING WRONG! That signal comes to you in the form of pain. If you're cutting bread and accidentally cut your finger, the pain signal stops you very quickly. If you didn't feel pain the instant you cut yourself, you might cut off your whole finger without even knowing it!

Does the pain serve any useful purpose while a cut is healing?

If you have a cut on some part of your body it will heal best if that part of the body doesn't move too much.

Moving a lot would keep the cells from growing together firmly. Pain is your body's way of keeping you from moving a part of your body that needs to heal. Every time you start to move it, ouch! And so you try to keep it still. When the wound has healed completely you no longer feel any pain when you move that part of the body.

What is a black and blue mark?

A black and blue mark is an injury that did not break the skin. But when you banged your arm or leg there *was* some bleeding—under the top layer of the skin. Your body stops this bleeding in the same way it stops bleeding from a cut in the skin: the blood thickens and forms a clot, so that the bleeding stops. But when you have a cut the blood you see is red, because it combines with oxygen in the air. The blood clotting under the skin loses its oxygen. It changes from a red color to blue, then to green and yellow as the blood cells are broken down. This gives it the colors you see when you get a bruise, or a black and blue mark.

What makes a black and blue mark go away?

Various body fluids gradually wash away the clotted blood under the skin and the black and blue mark disappears.

When you lose blood from a cut, do you end up with less blood in your body?

You may have a little less for a while. But your body quickly makes extra new blood to make up for the lost blood. You end up with as much blood as you had before.

Why do you sometimes need to get a tetanus shot when you've had a bad cut?

There is a particularly dangerous germ called tetanus that is often found living in the ground outdoors, but that may be carried indoors by people's muddy shoes. If this germ gets into the body through a deep cut it will cause a very serious disease called tetanus, or lockjaw. To keep you from getting tetanus, the doctor can give you a shot of medicine that builds up your body's antibodies against the tetanus germs.

Why are you more likely to get tetanus from a deep cut than a little scratch?

The tetanus germ is a special kind of creature that can only live and grow in places where there is *no* air or oxygen. In a deep, narrow wound where air cannot reach, the tetanus germ is much more likely to cause trouble. That is why it is a good idea to keep a deep, narrow wound open to air, and to try to wash it out very thoroughly.

What is a nosebleed?

A nosebleed is exactly what it sounds like: blood coming out of the nose.

What causes a nosebleed?

There are many small, thin, blood tubes in the lining of your nose. These can be broken easily. If you fall on your nose or have any sort of injury around your nose, you are likely to break some of these small tubes and get a nosebleed. You may even start a nosebleed by picking your nose. Sometimes getting very excited about something will make your heart pump blood faster. The extra strength of the blood rushing through those thin blood tubes in the nose may cause some of them to break and give you a nosebleed.

How long does a nosebleed last?

Most nosebleeds stop by themselves within ten minutes. They stop in the same way a cut stops bleeding:

the blood clots. But sometimes a nosebleed goes on longer. Then it is a good idea to try to stop it in some way.

Is there a good way of stopping a nosebleed?

Lying down helps stop a nosebleed sometimes. Something cold against the nose is also helpful. Putting a little bit of gauze or cotton or even kleenex into the nose for a few minutes will sometimes do the trick. But if a nosebleed doesn't stop fairly soon you should see a doctor.

Should you blow your nose right after you've had a nosebleed?

It's a good idea *not* to blow your nose for a while after you've had a nosebleed. The force of the blowing might disturb the clot and start the bleeding again.

6

I'm Sick to My Stomach: Stomachaches and Pains and Digestive Troubles

What is vomiting?

Throwing up, or vomiting, is the body's way of emptying the stomach very quickly, when necessary. Usually the food you eat stays in the stomach for a few hours while the stomach works at digesting it. When you vomit, the stomach can empty in a few minutes.

Why does the body ever need to empty the stomach quickly?

If there is something harmful in the stomach, either some germs that are causing trouble or something bad you ate, then it is useful to empty the stomach quickly.

Is getting rid of something harmful the only reason you vomit?

There is another reason why you sometimes vomit that has nothing to do with harmful things in your stomach. If you have real trouble in some other part of the body, an ear infection, for instance, your body may need all the energy it can get to fight the infection. Since a certain amount of your body's energy is needed to digest food in the stomach, you may vomit so that your body won't have to use its energy to digest food. When your stomach is empty then your body can use all its energies on fighting the infection.

Can seeing or smelling something awful, or thinking about something awful, make you vomit?

Yes. The motions of your stomach and intestines are controlled by nerves. Sometimes these nerves can be set off by particularly horrible sights or smells.

When you vomit, how does the food go uphill out of your stomach?

It may surprise you to learn that it is not gravity that makes the food you eat go down to the stomach. You can easily prove this by standing on your head against a wall and having somebody feed you a small piece of bread or a cookie. The food will still head for your stomach, even though it has to move "uphill" this time.

Whether you are right side up or upside down, the food that you eat is taken to the stomach by the action of small muscles along the walls of your esophagus, the tube that leads from the throat to the stomach. These muscles usually push the food in one direction only—toward the stomach.

But at certain times the brain sends a message to your stomach: REVERSE GEARS! A muscle closes off the bottom end of the stomach that leads to the intestine. The stomach muscles push very hard, and the squeezing forces the food in the only direction it will now go—up! The food comes out of the mouth again in whatever form it had in the stomach. That's what happens when you vomit.

Why does vomit taste so terrible?

Before you vomited, the food had a chance to mix with a very strong acid in your stomach called *hydrochloric* acid (hi-droe-klóre-ic). Some of the acid comes into your mouth with the undigested food when you vomit. The acid has a strong and nasty taste.

What is diarrhea?

Normally you move your bowels once or twice every day or two. When you have diarrhea (die-a-rée-a), you have to move your bowels much more often and what comes out is loose and watery.

What causes diarrhea?

Usually diarrhea is caused by harmful bacteria or viruses that have settled down in the intestine. They irritate the intestine and force it to get rid of its contents very quickly. Like the stomach in vomiting, the intestine tries to get rid of these harmful intruders by emptying quickly. But it doesn't work too well. Usually they stay and make trouble until other defenses of your body get to work at them.

Eating or drinking some harmful substance may cause diarrhea, too, if the substance manages to get past the stomach and into the intestine. In this case diarrhea will help get rid of that substance quickly and prevent it from harming your body's cells.

How does diarrhea work?

Food usually stays in the intestine for a few hours. During that time it is broken down by the strong juices of the intestine into a very simple liquid that can be used as food by all the cells of the body. A part of the food you eat, however, cannot be broken down into that simple liquid. That part is called the waste material. After all the usable parts of the food you eat have gone out of the intestine and into the blood, all that is left is the waste material. This is usually solid, because most of the liquids in the intestine can be used by the body, and therefore go back into the bloodstream.

When you have diarrhea, the intestine hasn't had a chance to finish its work on the food. It hasn't broken everything down into a simple liquid. When the intestine gets rid of everything in a hurry what comes out is some of the liquidy food that hasn't had a chance to get into the bloodstream, and the waste material, that hasn't had a chance to become solid, as well as some of the juices that the intestine has added to the food in order to digest it. That is why the bowel movement is so loose and watery when you have diarrhea.

How do you treat diarrhea?

The best treatment for diarrhea is to give the intestine a complete rest for a while by eating very little. Then it is a good idea to watch what you eat for a while until everything is working normally again. Some of the foods that are good to eat when you have diarrhea are ripe bananas, a scraped raw apple, boiled rice, and tea, water, or apple juice to drink.

Why do you burp?

You have two passageways leading away from your throat. One, the windpipe, leads air from the throat to the lungs. The other, the esophagus, leads food from the throat to the stomach. The windpipe has a special trapdoor at its entrance that keeps food from getting into your lungs when you breathe. But the food passageway has no trapdoor to keep air from getting in. Therefore if you gulp in air in some way when you eat or drink, a bubble of swallowed air forms. Usually this air bubble simply disappears into your body. But sometimes the bubble comes back up the food passageway. On its way out it makes a funny sound in the same way as a balloon makes a funny sound as the air runs out. This sound is a burp.

What is a hiccup?

The diaphragm between your chest and your stomach, usually goes up and down very regularly, pushing air in and out of your lungs. When you have the hiccups, your diaphragm has begun to behave in a very peculiar manner. Suddenly it starts to give out sudden little downward jerks, making you breathe in very suddenly over and over again. Those funny little jerks of the diaphragm are what we call the hiccups.

Why do you get the hiccups?

Nobody knows for sure why people get the hiccups. They may be caused by a small gas bubble in your stomach pressing against the diaphragm. We know that you are likely to get the hiccups if you bolt your food in a great hurry.

How do you get rid
of the hiccups?

Most hiccups go away by themselves within a few minutes. If the hiccups don't seem to be going away quickly, here are some cures that sometimes work: sip a glass of water very, very slowly; hold your breath for as long as you can; breathe into a paper bag for a minute or two. Getting somebody to scare you sometimes works, too!

What causes the pain when you have a
stomachache?

The pain of a stomachache is partly caused by gases pressing against pain nerves on the sides of your intestine and partly by the muscles of your intestine working too hard.

Is a stomachache always caused by an
infection in the intestines?

No. Some other things that give you a stomachache are appendicitis, hunger, and eating too much or too fast.

Being hungry is almost as unpleasant as
having a stomachache. How does
hunger work?

Most of the things that go on in your body work automatically. Your heart pumps blood. Your lungs take in air. Your stomach and intestines digest food. You don't have to stop or start anything. These things work by themselves.

You have to give the body the right fuel to make everything work right. That fuel is the food you eat. But your body doesn't take in food automatically. You have to eat food regularly to stay alive.

If you were to get so busy that you forgot to eat food, your body would soon be in a lot of trouble. But your body has a warning signal to keep you from forgetting to take in the food you need. That signal is HUNGER. Hunger is a very unpleasant feeling. And the more your body needs food, the more unpleasant that hungry feeling gets.

When your body needs more food, your brain sends the hunger signal: GO AND EAT SOMETHING RIGHT AWAY. When you've eaten enough to satisy your body's needs, the hungry feeling goes away. Now your brain sends another signal to keep you from eating *more* than you need. That signal is the full feeling you get at the end of a meal. It tells you: STOP EATING NOW. THAT'S ALL THE FOOD YOU NEED FOR A WHILE!

What are hunger pangs?

When there is food in the stomach, usually there are some gases trapped there as well. As the stomach muscles push in and out to mix the food with the digestive juices, the food acts as a sort of pillow. It protects the pain nerves on the walls of the stomach from the pressure of the gases. When there is no food in the stomach, the gases takes up most of the room there. The stomach muscles keep pushing in and out, and this makes the gases build up pressure. They push against the walls of the stomach each time the muscles push in and out. Each muscle movement causes a sharp pain. This is called a hunger pang.

Does thirst work the same way as hunger?

Yes, getting thirsty is your body's signal that it needs more liquids, just as getting hungry is the signal that the body needs more food. You lose liquids from your body in many natural ways—by breathing, urinating, and especially by sweating. The brain decides when your body needs more liquids and then sends a message to your mouth and throat: DRINK SOMETHING SOON! The greater your body's need for liquids, the thirstier you will feel.

What causes seasickness or car sickness?

Your sense of balance depends on some curved tubes in your inner ear. These tubes are partly filled with a liquid. Everytime you move that liquid moves. The tubes send a message to the brain, telling it which way you're moving. Then the brain sends back messages to certain muscles in your body to make you keep your balance perfectly. For instance, when you lean way over to the left, the liquid in the ear tube moves over to the left in the tube. This sends a message to the brain: BALANCE TO THE LEFT! Then the proper muscles will help you keep your balance, even when leaning way over to the left.

But when you are moving in a boat or a car (or a plane or

any other moving thing), the liquid in the ear tubes will keep moving in the way the boat is moving, even while you are sitting completely still and don't need any extra muscle work to keep your balance. The brain gets a wrong message from the ear and the wrong muscles begin to work. This creates a lot of confusion in your brain, which somehow causes the dizziness and sick-to-the-stomach feeling you call being carsick or seasick.

After a while, however, your brain usually gets used to the situation. It starts sending the right messages again, in spite of the movement of the boat or car. Then you no longer feel sick.

Why do some people get carsick or seasick, and others don't?

Some people's bodies adjust almost immediately to the movement of a car or boat or plane. They do not get the mixed-up signals that cause travel sickness. They hardly ever get sick in cars or boats or planes. Other people's bodies seem especially sensitive to this sort of trouble.

7

Sneezles, Wheezles, Colds, and the Flu: Common Infections

What is an infection?

An infection is a condition caused by germs. Colds and the flu are very common infections.

What is a cold?

A cold, sometimes called the common cold, is an *infection* of the nose and throat and sometimes of the air passages that lead to the lungs. Almost everybody gets a cold once in a while.

What kind of germs cause a cold?

A cold is caused by a virus. But there is not just one single kind of virus that causes colds. There are many different viruses that cause colds.

Why can you catch colds over and over again while you get some sicknesses like the measles or mumps only once?

Sicknesses like the mumps are caused by one and only one kind of germ. When you are sick with the mumps, your body begins to make quantities of a special kind of substance called an *antibody*. These antibodies have one big job: to fight against the mumps germs and keep them from harming you. The mumps antibodies, however, will only work against mumps germs. They will not fight against measles or chicken-pox germs. Your body makes separate antibodies for each sickness at the time that you have that sickness. But once your body has made antibodies against a sickness, they will stay in your blood even after you are well from the sickness. They will keep you from ever getting that sickness again.

Every time you catch a cold, your body also makes antibodies against the cold virus that is making you sick. But sometimes the "cold" antibodies don't last forever. And also, since there are many kinds of viruses that cause colds, the antibodies from the last time you had a cold may not work against the new virus that is causing your new cold. That's one reason why you catch colds so many times: each cold may be caused by a new virus for which you have no antibodies in your blood.

Why do children catch more colds than grown-ups?

When you are very young you can catch a cold from any of the many cold viruses that are around. Then each time you catch a cold you will build up antibodies against that particular virus that is causing your cold. By the time you're a grown-up you will have antibodies against a great many different viruses in your blood, waiting to protect you from those viruses if they come around. That will keep you from getting as many colds as you had when you were a child.

Why do you get a runny nose when you have a cold?

The cells that make up the lining of your nose are able to make a sticky liquid called mucus. (See p. 14, What happens if germs get into the body through the nose?) When you have a cold, a large number of germs have somehow managed to settle down in the lining of your nose. The cells that make up the lining of your nose try to get rid of these germs by making more and more mucus. Pretty soon there is too much mucus to slowly drip down from your nose to your throat the way mucus usually does when you *don't* have a cold. Now some of it overflows and comes running out of the nose. That's how you get a runny nose.

When you have a runny nose, why is the liquid that comes out thin and watery sometimes and thick and yellowish other times?

The thin, watery liquid is plain mucus. The thick yellowish stuff is called pus (see page 24).

Why does pus come out of your nose when you have a cold?

When you have a cold your body sends white blood cells to fight the germs that have settled in your nose. As a result of this fight some pus is left over in the nose. This is the thick yellowish stuff that comes out of your nose when you have a cold. You may not like having a stuffy, clogged-up nose, but next time you have one remember that the pus is a sure sign that your body's defense system is working hard to keep you out of trouble with germs.

What causes a sore throat?

Various things cause a sore throat. Sometimes yelling too hard will give you a sore throat, or drinking something too hot. But usually a sore throat is caused by germs that have settled down to grow in the lining of your throat or in your tonsils. Your body fights to get rid of these germs in its usual way—inflammation (see p.6). An extra supply of blood with germ-killing white blood cells rushes to the spot. This extra blood causes the redness and swelling of a sore throat. The swelling pushes against the many pain nerves in the throat and causes the pain that you feel when you have a sore throat.

What is a strep throat?

A strep throat is an infection in the throat caused by special bacteria called *streptococci* (strep-toe-cóck-eye).

A strep throat is dangerous because it can lead to more dangerous illnesses such as rheumatic fever. That is why it is important not to let those strep bacteria stay in the throat for long. It is important to treat strep throats right away with antibiotics. And it is especially important to take those medicines for as long as the doctor tells you to take them, even after you feel quite well and go back to school. You usually have to take antibiotics for about ten days after you have had a strep throat, so that the strep germs will be completely killed.

Why do you sometimes get a hoarse voice when you have a cold?

Inside your throat is a wonderful contraption called the *larynx* (lá-rinks) or voice box. The air you breathe passes through the voice box on its way to the lungs. It is the movement of air across the vocal cords stretching across the opening of the voice box that makes sounds come out when you speak. The thicker your vocal cords, the lower the sound they make when the air moves across them (just as the thicker strings of a violin or cello make lower sounds when you pluck them than the thinner strings). Men have thicker vocal cords than women; that's why men's voices are lower.

When you have a cold, germs sometimes settle down around the voice box. Your body begins to fight these germs in its usual way, by rushing blood with germ-killing white blood cells to the spot. This makes the vocal cords swell up and get thicker. The vocal cords also give off extra mucus to fight the germs. This extra mucus muffles the sounds you make when you speak. The combination of the thicker vocal cords and the extra mucus make your voice sound low and hoarse when you have a cold.

Why do you cough when you have a cold?

Sometimes when you have a cold, germs settle down to grow along the passageway from your throat to your lungs. The cells that line the passageway begin to make more sticky mucus to catch the germs and keep them from getting to the lungs. But when there is a lot of mucus in the air passageway, it is harder for air to get into the lungs. Coughing is your body's way of clearing the air passageway. The mucus is coughed up out of the passageway and into the throat. Then it is swallowed. The germs caught in the mucus are quickly killed by the strong acids in the stomach.

How does coughing work?

When you need to cough, your brain sends a signal to some of the muscles you use in breathing. Those muscles tighten up and pull in very hard. At the same time your vocal cords in your throat stay closed up very tightly. Suddenly the vocal cords open up. The air that has been building up is now blasted out of the lungs at a great speed. Sometimes the air goes as fast as 125 miles an hour! That air blasting out of the lungs makes a noise as it goes through the vocal cords. That noise is a cough.

Why do you sneeze when you have a cold?

A sneeze helps clear up the passageway from the nose to the lungs and makes breathing easier. When you have a cold, the germs in your nose and the extra mucus in your nose may tickle and bother some little nerve endings at the back of the nose. They send a quick message to the brain: CLEARING UP NEEDED! The brain sends a message back: KERCHOO!

How does sneezing work?

A sneeze is something like a cough, with a big blast of air coming out of the lungs. But when you sneeze your tongue automatically goes up against the top of your mouth. This pushes most of the air out through your nose. In this way most of the force of the blast is pushed through the nose canal. This helps clear your nose when you have a cold. Your brain will also send the sneeze signal when some irritating little particle like dust gets into the nose.

Does the nose make mucus even when you don't have a cold?

The cells inside your nose are busy making mucus all the time. There is always a little bit of mucus going from your nose to your throat. But you hardly notice the mucus in your nose when you don't have a cold because there's such a small amount of it. It's always there though. Try snuffling in and clearing your nose as if you had a cold, and then swallow hard. You will feel a little mucus come down into your throat.

How much mucus does the nose make every day?

Even when you don't have a cold, the nose makes almost a quart of liquid mucus every single day!

Where does all that liquid come from?

There are tiny *glands* inside the lining of your nose. These glands squeeze liquid out of your bloodstream and use it to make mucus.

Why does everything taste so strange and funny when you have a cold?

What you taste when you eat depends on two things: the flavor of the food and also its smell. When you have a cold all the extra mucus in your nose blocks up many of the smelling nerves in your nose. This means that only your tasting nerves are working as you eat. This makes eating very different from the times when both your taste and smell nerves work together.

Why do you get an earache?

An earache is usually the result of an ear infection.

What is an ear infection?

An ear infection is a sickness caused by germs that have settled down to live and multiply inside the ear.

How do germs get inside the ear?

There is a canal that connects the inside of your ear with your throat. This is called the eustachian tube (you-stay-shun). If you have a cold or an infection of some sort inside your throat, germs can sometimes get into the ear by means of the eustachian tube.

What happens when you have an ear infection?

The swelling from your cold or throat infection blocks up the eustachian tube that leads from the ear to the throat. Now any germs that may be in the ear find it much easier to settle down and cause trouble. Fluid from the inflammation caused by the ear infection collects in the ear, causing pain. Finally, it may cause the eardrum to burst. This may cause some hearing loss.

Why do you take antibiotics when you have an ear infection?

Most ear infections are caused by bacteria. These can be killed by antibiotics very quickly, much more quickly than waiting for your body to fight the infection on its own. Without antibiotics, you might end up with a burst eardrum and hearing loss.

Can blowing your nose the wrong way cause ear infections?

If you have a cold, pinching one nostril shut and blowing your nose hard may force some infected material through the eustachian tube into the ear. This may start an ear infection. It is always best to blow your nose through both nostrils at the same time.

Why do children get so many more ear infections than grown-ups?

The shape of the eustachian tube is different in children's bodies than in the grown-up body, and is more likely to get blocked up when you have a cold. This makes it much easier for germs to find their way into the ear. In grown-ups, germs are much more likely to drain harmlessly into the throat.

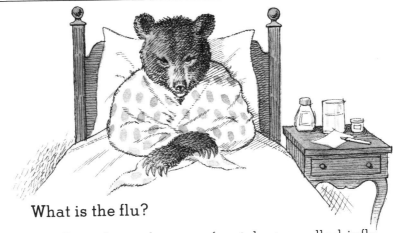

What is the flu?

The flu is the nickname of a sickness called influenza. It is something like a cold, except much worse. You may have a fever, a sore throat, and a generally achy feeling all over, as well as the regular cold symptoms: a runny nose, a cough, and a hoarse voice.

What causes the flu?

The flu is caused by a virus. But there are many different viruses that cause the flu, just as there are different viruses that cause colds. That's why you can catch the flu more than one time. (See page 43, Why can you catch colds many times?)

How do you catch the flu?

You catch the flu by being with someone who is already infected with the flu virus. When that person coughs or sneezes, the viruses float around in the air on little droplets of water. When you breathe in, those droplets with their load of viruses come into your body through your nose or mouth.

Do any medicines help when you have the flu?

There are no medicines that will cure the common virus infections. The body has to fight its own battle against viruses without any help from medicines. The best thing you can do when you have the flu is to get plenty of rest and drink plenty of liquids.

Why does getting plenty of rest help when you have the flu?

When your body is fighting an infection it needs to use as much energy as possible in the fight. When you are resting your body does not need much energy. All the energy made by your body's cells can go into fighting the germs that are making you sick. But when you run around and play actively a great deal of energy has to go toward making your muscles move and pumping extra oxygen and blood throughout your body. This makes it harder for your body to fight the germs. It will take your body longer to win its fight against the infection.

Why does drinking liquids help when you have the flu or any other infection?

When you have an infection your body makes much more mucus than usual to try to get rid of the germs. Drinking extra liquids helps the body make more mucus. Also, you lose water when you have a fever. You need to replace this by drinking more than usual when you are sick.

8

Chicken Pox, Mumps, and All That: Other Sicknesses Caused by Germs

What is the chicken pox?

Chicken pox is a very common sickness that is caused by a virus. It is very contagious and is mostly caught by children.

What happens when you catch the chicken pox?

Chicken pox starts like many other sicknesses: you don't feel well and you have a fever. A day or two later a rash begins to appear on different parts of the body. The rash is made up of tiny pimples that slowly grow into small blisters. The blisters soon break and form a red crust. The rash may continue to show up in new places for about four days from the time it began. Then the little blisters begin to heal. The temperature goes back to normal. Chicken pox is over.

Why does the chicken-pox virus cause one special kind of rash and other viruses cause different rashes?

Different viruses choose to live in different parts of the body. The viruses that cause rashes live in different layers of the skin. The chicken-pox virus always chooses to live and multiply under the very top layer of skin. The virus destroys cells and causes the top layer of skin to separate from the next layer. This causes the chicken-pox blisters. Other viruses that cause other diseases choose to live in lower layers of the skin. They cause very different rashes to appear.

Do the pimples and blisters from chicken pox hurt?

No, but they *do* itch. That is the worst part of having chicken pox, because when something itches you want to scratch it. But it is very important not to scratch the chicken-pox blisters because they could get infected with different germs. Then it would take much longer for them to heal, and they might leave scars behind. If you don't scratch the chicken-pox blisters, though, you won't have any scars at all.

How do you catch the chicken pox?

You catch the chicken pox by coming near somebody else who is sick with the chicken pox. But somebody who is about to come down with chicken pox can still pass down the sickness to you, even before he breaks out in a rash. That's why it's hard to keep from catching it. If you play with a friend one day and he seems perfectly well, but the next day he comes down with chicken pox, he has already passed it on to you the day before. You will probably get the chicken pox, if you've never had it before. But once you have the chicken pox you can never catch it again.

If you come near someone with chicken pox, how soon will you come down with the sickness?

It takes about two or three weeks from the time you first come near the chicken-pox germs for you to show the first signs of the sickness.

Why does it take so long?

It takes fourteen to twenty-one days for the chicken-pox virus to get a hold inside your body and make you sick. That period of time between your first meeting with a germ and the first signs of sickness is called the *incubation* (in-kew-báy-shun) period.

Is there any medicine that helps when you have the chicken pox?

There is no medicine yet that will fight and kill the common viruses. But your body does a perfectly good job of fighting the chicken-pox viruses by itself. That's why it is not considered a serious sickness. If the itching gets too bad though there are medicines and lotions that help the itching.

What is mumps?

Mumps is a sickness caused by a virus that makes itself at home in one special place: in the *glands* at the sides and back of the mouth which make the saliva in your mouth. (Saliva is the liquid in your mouth that forms "spit".)

What happens when you get mumps?

Mumps will usually start with a fever and a head-ache, like many other sicknesses. Then you start to feel a swelling, usually on one side of your face only, but some-times on both. The swelling is behind the jaw, just under the ears. You begin to look a little funny, a bit like a chipmunk with a cheek full of seeds. But you don't *feel* it's very funny, because the swelling makes chewing and eating and even just swallowing saliva very painful. The swelling of mumps may last about a week or even ten days. Finally the fever goes away, the swelling goes down, and you feel well again. The mumps are finished.

How do you catch mumps?

You catch the mumps from somebody else who has the mumps. You can catch the sickness from somebody a whole week before they show any signs of sickness or swelling, though. They already *have* the mumps germs growing inside them, but they don't know it. By the time they start showing real signs of the mumps it's too late for you to stay away—you've already caught it!

How long does it take from the time you first come near somebody with mumps to the time you come down with mumps yourself?

The *incubation period* of mumps germs is about three weeks. That's how long it takes for the mumps germs to grow inside you until your body starts fighting them with *inflammation* and other defenses.

When you get mumps on one side of your face, can you get it again some other time on the other side?

No. When you get mumps on either side, your body develops *antibodies* against the mumps virus. Those antibodies stay in your body and keep you from getting mumps ever again. (See Why can you catch colds over and over again . . . , page 43.)

Are there any medicines that help your body fight mumps?

As with other virus sicknesses, the mumps cannot be helped by taking any medicines. The same old things help you when you have the mumps: drinking plenty of liquids and getting plenty of rest.

Is mumps a very bad sickness? Why do children get mumps shots to keep from getting it?

Mumps is a very mild sickness when children catch it. But when grownups catch the mumps it can be much more serious for them. That is one reason why children get shots against the mumps—to keep grownups from catching it from them. Also, children who get mumps shots will never be in danger of catching the mumps when *they* grow up.

What is Rubella?

Rubella (roo-bell-la) is a mild disease caused by a virus. It is also sometimes called German measles.

What happens when you catch Rubella?

The sickness often starts with a headache and a few cold *symptoms* such as a runny nose. Sometimes there is a low fever, not higher than 102 degrees, but sometimes there is no fever at all when you have Rubella. A day or two after you start feeling sick a splotchy rash begins to appear on the body. It usually starts on the face and spreads downward. After four or five days the rash begins to disappear and Rubella is over. But sometimes there is almost no rash when you have Rubella and you hardly feel sick at all. Many people have Rubella and don't even know it! Rubella is almost always a very mild disease when children catch it.

If Rubella is such a mild disease, why do children get shots to keep from catching it?

Rubella is almost never a serious disease for children. It doesn't bother most grownups much either, if they catch it. But there is one group of people for whom Rubella is a very serious and dangerous sickness: unborn babies! When a mother who is expecting a baby catches Rubella, the unborn baby growing inside her catches the sickness, too. And while the viruses don't do anything bad to the mother, they can do some terrible things to the unborn baby. When the baby is born it may be deaf, or blind, or have some other things wrong with it. It is important to keep children from catching Rubella because they can easily spread it to mothers who are expecting babies. That's why almost all children get Rubella shots now.

Once you have been exposed to someone with Rubella, how long will it take you to come down with the sickness (if you haven't had the Rubella shots)?

The incubation period of Rubella is fourteen to sixteen days. But even before you show any signs of sickness you can pass it on to somebody else.

Once you've had Rubella, can you ever catch it again?

No. Your body's antibodies against the Rubella virus made while you have the sickness will keep you from ever catching it again.

What is pneumonia?

Pneumonia (noo-mōe-nee-a) is a sickness caused by viruses or bacteria that somehow manage to get into the lungs and settle down to live and multiply there. The body's fight against these unwanted germs causes the symptoms of pneumonia. But there are also some kinds of pneumonia that are not caused by any germs at all!

What happens when you get pneumonia caused by viruses or bacteria?

When the germs settle down in the lungs, the body fights them in its usual way—inflammation! A larger supply of blood with the white blood cell germ-killers rushes to the lungs. The extra blood makes everything swell and get puffy. The cells in the lungs also make a great deal more of the sticky mucus to try to trap the troublesome germs. This extra mucus clogs up parts of the lungs. The swelling and the extra mucus make you cough a lot in order to be able to breathe. And the swelling sometimes pushes against pain nerves in the chest. This makes your whole chest ache.

How can you get pneumonia that is *not* caused by germs?

Usually when you eat, a little trapdoor on top of your windpipe shuts nice and tight. This keeps any food from getting into your lungs instead of into your stomach. But if you breathe in something very irritating, like tiny bits of powder, or if you run and jump wildly while eating, then the trap door won't close the right way. Some little bits of powder or food may get into your lungs. These little bits that don't belong there will cause pneumonia.

How does getting something into the lungs that doesn't belong there cause pneumonia?

The little bits of powder or food stay in the lungs and begin to irritate the very delicate cells of the lungs. The body fights back against these foreigners in the lungs in the same way it fights against germs—inflammation! It sends out its troops to get rid of the intruders. Extra blood causes swelling. Extra mucus clogs up parts of the lungs. You have all the symptoms of pneumonia.

9

Operation! Having Your Tonsils or Appendix Taken Out

I HAVE TO HAVE MY TONSILS OUT!

What are tonsils?

Tonsils are two special kinds of germ traps called *lymph* (limf) that are found at the back of your mouth.

What are lymph nodes?

Lymph nodes are part of your body's defense system against germs. They appear in various parts of the body, especially in the neck and armpits. They help trap germs and produce great quantities of extra white blood cells to kill germs.

What is tonsillitis?

Tonsillitis is an *infection* of the tonsils.

What happens when you have tonsillitis?

When germs begin to grow in the tonsils the body's natural defense system gets to work to fight the germs. Extra blood with germ-killing white blood cells rushes to the spot. This makes the tonsils swell and get larger. The swelling pushes against pain nerves in the throat. This causes you to feel a bad sore throat. Sometimes other body defenses begin to work and you have a fever with tonsillitis. The swollen tonsils also make it hard for you to swallow or do much talking.

Are there any medicines that help your body fight tonsillitis?

Yes, *antibiotics* such as penicillin will help cure tonsillitis *if* the germs causing it are bacteria. But if it is a virus causing the trouble, then antibiotics won't help at all.

How can you tell if your tonsillitis is caused by bacteria or a virus?

Your doctor can tell easily by taking a throat *culture*. This is done by touching the lining of your throat with a cotton swab stick to get a sample of the germs in your throat. Then the germs from the swab stick are put in a place with just the right conditions for them to live and multiply well. When they have grown for a while the doctor can look at them under a microscope to see what kind of germs they are.

Can you get tonsillitis more than once?

Yes, like a cold or the flu, you can get tonsillitis over and over again. In fact, some children seem to get tonsillitis all the time. This is one reason why doctors sometimes suggest that the tonsils be taken out of the body in an operation. The tonsils are sometimes taken out when something is wrong with the *adenoids* (á-de-noyds) and *they* need to be taken out.

What are the adenoids?

Adenoids are also lymph nodes, somewhat like the tonsils but about half their size. They lie along the back wall of the throat at around the place where the passage to the nose starts. You cannot see the adenoids even when you open your mouth very wide. They lie just out of sight.

What can go wrong with the adenoids?

The adenoids, like the tonsils, can become infected by germs. Then they swell up. This can make normal breathing through the nose difficult, causing you to breathe mostly through your mouth. When your adenoids are swollen you usually snore at night as you breathe in your sleep. A more serious problem with swollen adenoids is that they may block the eustachian tube that leads from the ears to the throat. This may cause serious trouble for the ears and you might end up with hearing damage. This is the main reason why adenoids sometimes need to be taken out.

If tonsils and adenoids are lymph nodes that are useful, why do they sometimes take them out in an operation?

You have many other lymph nodes in your body that serve the same purpose as the tonsils and adenoids. You can certainly live very well without them. But since doctors have begun to realize that tonsils and adenoids are not as useless as they once believed, they don't take them out as often as in the past.

Can your regular doctor take out your tonsils and adenoids?

No, this operation must be done by a specialist—a doctor with special training in problems of the ear, nose, and throat. He is usually called an E-N-T doctor, although his actual title is an *otolaryngologist* (ó-toe-la-ring-gól-o-gist).

Do you have to go to the hospital to have your tonsils and adenoids taken out?

A number of years ago some doctors took out children's tonsils and adenoids right in their offices. Sometimes they did the operation for all the children in a family one after another on the same day, even if they all didn't need the operation! Today tonsils and adenoids are almost never taken out if it isn't absolutely necessary and the operation is always done in a hospital.

How does the doctor take out the tonsils and adenoids?

He cuts them off quite easily with a sharp little instrument. It leaves a small wound that heals by itself.

Does it hurt to have your tonsils and adenoids taken out?

Before the doctor does the operation to take out your tonsils and adenoids he gives you a kind of medicine that puts you completely to sleep. This medicine is called an *anesthetic* (a-nes-théh-tic) from a Greek word meaning *no feeling*. And that's exactly what the anesthetic does: it causes you to have no feeling and no pain while you are sleeping and the operation is taking place.

How does the doctor give you the anesthetic that puts you to sleep?

Sometimes you get the medicine in an injection. Within a few seconds the medicine enters your blood and travels to the brain, where it puts you to sleep. Sometimes you breathe in a special gas that also puts you to sleep very quickly.

Does your throat hurt after the operation?

Your throat will be quite sore for a while until the wound from the operation heals.

Can the tonsils grow back?

The tonsils may grow back a little bit, but almost never enough to cause any trouble ever again.

Can you eat anything you want after you've had your tonsils and adenoids taken out?

Since your throat feels very sore after the operation you usually will feel better eating only very soft, easily swallowed foods such as jello, custard, mashed potatoes, and best of all, lots of ice cream and sherbet. The coldness of ice cream seems to make the sore throat feel better. Also, soft foods will not irritate the wound, giving it a chance to heal properly.

How soon after the operation can you be up and about again?

It usually takes about ten days to get back to normal after an operation to take out the tonsils and adenoids. But even after that it is a good idea to take it easy for another few weeks while the body gets back all its strength.

OUCH! MY APPENDIX HURTS!

What is appendicitis?

Appendicitis is an infection of a part of your body called the appendix. When you have appendicitis the appendix swells up to several times its usual size.

Where is the appendix in your body and what does it do?

The appendix is a small, fingerlike part of your body, sticking out of your large intestine. It is somewhere on the lower right side of your body, below your belly button. Unlike all the other various parts of your body that seem to serve some useful purpose, the appendix seems to do absolutely no good at all in your body. It just sits there. And sometimes it causes a lot of trouble.

What happens when you have appendicitis?

Appendicitis usually starts as a bad stomachache. You have cramps and pains all over, with a feeling of nausea, followed by vomiting. After a while the pain usually begins to feel much worse in the lower right side of your body.

How can you tell if you have appendicitis or just a bad stomachache?

A doctor has ways of knowing whether you have appendicitis or some other stomach troubles. The doctor will feel the area around your stomach when he suspects appendicitis. He can usually feel a difference in the muscles around the appendix if that is what's causing the trouble. But the best way to make sure that the problem is appendicitis is to take a white blood cell count. The doctor can take a small sample of your blood. He has a way of counting how many white blood cells there are in your blood. If he counts a great many more white blood cells than there usually are, that is a sure sign that you have an infection somewhere in your body. The bad pain in your stomach, combined with the evidence of the extra high white blood cell count makes the doctor quite sure that the problem is appendicitis.

Why do you need to have your appendix taken out when you have appendicitis?

When the appendix is infected it begins to swell. The fight of the white blood cells and the germs infecting the appendix produces some pus which collects inside the appendix. If the appendix is not removed quite soon after the infection starts, then the swelling and the collected pus might soon make the appendix burst open. Then the germs would spread to a much greater area of the body and cause a great deal of trouble. Since the appendix is a useless part of your body, the simplest way to take care of an infected appendix is to take it out of the body altogether.

Can your regular doctor take out your appendix?

No, a special doctor called a *surgeon* (śir-djun) is needed to do the operation.

Does it hurt to have your appendix taken out?

You are given an anesthetic to put you to sleep while the doctor takes out your appendix. You don't feel anything at all during the operation.

How does the surgeon actually remove the appendix?

The surgeon cuts a small opening through the skin on the lower right side of your body. Then he simply cuts off the appendix with a sharp little instrument. He stitches up the wound so that it will heal quickly, using a special kind of thread that will eventually melt away into the body. After he has removed the appendix and stitched up the wound, he then sews up the opening in the skin. This will allow the wound in the skin to heal quickly and evenly.

Does the scar from the operation stay forever?

Yes, the scar will never go away entirely. But it will look less obvious after a while. At first the scar will look very red, but it will get lighter and lighter as time goes by. Eventually it will hardly show at all. But the skin where the scar is will always look a little different from the regular skin around it.

Can the scar from the operation ever split open, letting everything come out?

Once the scar has healed it never splits open again. The scar material is at least as strong as the surrounding skin.

How soon can you get out of bed after you have your appendix taken out?

Usually you can get up for a little while the very next day!

How soon can you leave the hospital after the operation?

Usually you are ready to go home from the hospital in less than a week.

How soon after the operation can you be up and around again?

Usually you can go back to school three or four weeks after you have your appendix taken out. But you have to take it easy and not play any rough games or do any hard physical activity for about three or four weeks more.

Can you get appendicitis again after your appendix has been taken out?

No, the appendix is out for good, and without an appendix you cannot have appendicitis.

Can you get well from appendicitis without having your appendix taken out?

Yes, antibiotics like penicillin will sometimes help your body get rid of an infection in the appendix, just as they help fight infections in other parts of the body. But the appendix is likely to get infected again. Since it is a useless part of the body it is usually better to get rid of it right away when you have appendicitis.

10 All Sorts of Skin Troubles

SKIN TROUBLES CAUSED BY GERMS

What is a pimple or a boil?

A pimple or a boil is a raised spot or lump that is filled with pus. The pus is a sign that there is an infection causing the trouble.

What causes a pimple to form?

Your skin is covered all over with tiny hairs. At the base of each hair is a tiny gland that lets out a special oil. This oil helps soften the skin and keeps it from cracking. But sometimes one of those tiny glands becomes clogged up. The oil stays inside and cannot get out. When it gets too full of oil it bursts open. This injures some of the cells around it. Germs can then come in under the skin, just at the place where the hair comes out of the skin. This causes the pimple.

What makes a pimple swell up and turn red?

When cells are injured the body reacts with its usual defense—inflammation. Extra blood rushes to the spot. The nearby cells leak extra fluid. This causes the swelling of a boil or pimple. The extra blood gives the pimple its red color.

What makes a pimple or a boil go away?

Sometimes a pimple or a boil bursts open. The pus drains out, getting rid of the germs. Then repair cells fix up the injury. Sometimes the inflammation itself takes care of the infection without the pimple bursting. The swelling and redness then slowly disappear and pretty soon the pimple is gone.

What is a cold sore?

A cold sore is a painful red spot that appears around the lips and sometimes at the base of the nose. The spot gets swollen and oozy and usually lasts for a week or two. When it begins to heal a scab forms. The scab falls off when the sore is completely healed beneath it.

What causes a cold sore?

The cold sore is caused by a very common virus that works in a fascinating way. After the first time you get an infection with the cold sore virus, it sneaks into a nerve inside the lining of the mouth. It travels up that nerve to its end, somewhere behind your eye in your skull. There it sits and waits, although you have no idea it's there. Then some time when you are sick with a cold or some other sickness and your body is too busy fighting other germs to worry about the cold sore virus, it sneaks back down the nerve and comes out around your lip or nose. There it bothers you by causing a cold sore.

What is a wart?

A wart is a little growth on the skin that is caused by a virus infection. The action of the virus irritates the underlayers of the skin and makes them grow a thick, protective covering. This thickening of the skin causes the wart.

What makes a wart go away?

People used to believe that magic would cure warts. Here is one of the old spells people used to believe would cure warts.

Take the skins of two dead cats. Go to a graveyard at

midnight and swing the cat skins over your head three times. Your warts will be gone by morning!

In fact, the only sure way to get rid of a wart is to have it removed by a doctor.

Can you get warts from touching a frog or a toad?

No, that's just a superstition.

How are warts removed by a doctor?

A doctor uses an electric needle or a strong acid to burn the wart away. But first he gives you some anesthesia (pain-killer) so that you don't feel any pain while he removes the wart.

Can a wart come back after a doctor has removed it?

Yes, warts do come back sometimes. That's why doctors usually leave warts alone and hope that they'll go away by themselves. They often do.

SKIN TROUBLES NOT CAUSED BY GERMS

What is a blister?

Your skin is made of three separate layers. A blister is a bubble of watery liquid that lies just under the thin, top layer of your skin. The liquid makes the skin above it puff out.

What causes a blister?

Blisters are caused by some injury to the cells in the second layer of skin. A burn or a tight shoe rubbing against the skin will hurt or destroy some cells in the second layer of skin. The body reacts with inflammation. The blood tubes in the area leak out extra liquid. This extra liquid is what you find in a blister. Meanwhile, the tough top layer of skin has not broken. This holds the liquid in one place. The extra liquid covers the injured spot and keeps germs from growing there. It also takes away the injured cells so that new cells will grow in their place. When the new cells have grown, the blister disappears.

What happens if you break a blister?

The unbroken roof of a blister helps prevent infection. If you break the blister germs are able to get into the wound and start trouble.

What is a callus?

The word *callus* means hard skin in Latin, and that's exactly what a callus is. When some parts of the skin get a lot of wear and tear, rubbing and scraping, the body has a special way of protecting the skin in those places from wearing out. The body gradually makes the top layer of skin grow thicker and thicker at those places. This thicker-than-usual skin is called a callus. It keeps parts of the body that get hard use, like the soles of your feet or the palms of your hand, from getting worn through quickly.

What are goose-pimples or goose-bumps and why do you get them?

There is hair on almost all parts of your skin except for the palms, soles, toes and lips. These hairs may be so fine and light that you can hardly see them, but they are there. At the base of every single little hair is a tiny muscle cell. When your skin gets cold this muscle tightens up in order to warm up your skin temperature. This makes the hair stand up on your skin, causing a little bump. This is called a goose-pimple or goose-bump.

Why do you sometimes get goose-pimples when you're frightened?

When you get a scare your body sometimes lets out a special chemical called *adrenaline* (a-drén-a-lin) that helps you manage in emergencies. Like cold weather, this chemical makes those tiny hair muscles tighten up. That's why you sometimes get goose-pimples when you're frightened.

Why does your skin get blue when you're cold, especially if you've been swimming too long?

When you get cold your body does some special things to keep your body temperature from getting too low. The little blood tubes directly under the top layer of skin begin to get narrower and tighter. This keeps in more heat and keeps you from getting too cold. But when these tubes are narrower the blood cannot move through them at the usual speed. Now it has to move much more slowly. This gives most of the oxygen in the blood a chance to leave the blood and go into the body's cells, where it is needed to make energy.

Now, it is the oxygen in the blood that gives it its bright red color. When most of the oxygen has left the blood it takes on a bluish color. This bluish color shows through the top layer of skin and gives it a bluish color all over. When you warm up you will quickly lose that bluish color. That is because fresh blood loaded with oxygen and colored bright red is now traveling through the tiny blood tubes at the usual speed.

What makes the skin swell up and form a bump when you get a mosquito bite?

When the stinger of a mosquito breaks your skin, your body lets out a little of that chemical histamine that is always at work in allergic reactions. The histamine makes the cells around it leak out extra fluid. This causes the skin to form a bump.

Why does a mosquito bite itch?

That same chemical, histamine, irritates some pain nerves in the area. Those nerves cause you to feel itchy. If the irritation were stronger you would feel pain. But a mild irritation causes the nerves to send an itch message.

What is a burn?

The cells of your body need to be just the right temperature to stay alive and well. If the temperature gets even a little bit hotter than usual, the cells will be harmed. The higher the temperature, the worse damage will happen to the cells. Damage caused by too high a temperature applied to the body's cells is called a burn.

Why do you sometimes get a blister when you burn yourself?

The heat destroys the connection between the layers of skin. Fluid which leaks out of blood tubes in the area fills up the space. This causes a blister.

What is a sunburn?

The strong rays of the sun can damage and destroy living cells of the body in the same way as flames of a fire can. When cells have been damaged by the sun's rays the injury is called a sunburn.

Why don't you get a sunburn every time you go out in the sun?

Whether you get a sunburn or not depends upon the time of day, the season of the year, and on your skin's natural protection against sunburn.

How does the time of day and season of year make a difference?

When the sun is low in the sky in the morning or in the evening, most of the burning rays are lost in the atmosphere. This keeps you from getting a sunburn.

In the winter, early spring, and late fall, our part of the earth is tipped away from the sun and the rays are longer. You are not likely to get a sunburn then. But in the summer and especially around the middle of the day, the sun's rays can strike your body most directly. You are most likely to get a sunburn.

What is your skin's natural protection against sunburn?

Whether you get a sunburn or not depends a lot on the color of your skin. If your skin is dark brown or black it contains a large quantity of a chemical called *melanin* (mél-luh-nin). Melanin is a very useful thing to have in your skin. It can soak up many of the harmful rays of the sun without allowing any cells of the body to be damaged. People with a lot of melanin in the skin can stay in the sun for a long time without any danger of sunburn.

But if your skin is very pale and light, it does not have much melanin in it. Then there is nothing to protect it from getting burned by the hot rays of the sun.

Does that mean that people with light skins can never stay in the sun without getting a sunburn?

If you have light skin there is a good way to build up more melanin in your skin: GET A SUNTAN! Every time you stay in the sun for a short period of time your skin automatically makes a little melanin. This makes your skin a little darker. Then you stay in the sun a little longer. You build up even more melanin. Each time your skin gets a little darker, it gains more protection from the sun. When your skin is quite dark you have a suntan. Now your skin is protected against the burning rays of the sun.

Once you have a good suntan, are you permanently protected against sunburn?

People with naturally dark or black skin do not ever lose their melanin from their skin. But if your skin is light and you have made more melanin in your skin by gradually getting a suntan, that melanin will only stay in your skin if you continue to spend long periods of time in the sun. When you stay out of the sun for a while, your suntan will fade as the melanin leaves your skin. Then you are in danger of getting a sunburn again if you go out into the sun.

Can everybody get a suntan?

No, some people who have very light skin, especially blondes and redheads, cannot seem to make much melanin in their skin even if they try to get a gradual suntan. They will always burn if they stay in the hot sun for too long.

What are freckles?

Freckles are little spots of melanin on the face and body. When some people get sunlight on their skin they seem to produce melanin in little spots instead of tanning evenly. These people will get more freckles when they stay in the sun a lot. Then the freckles will fade, just as a suntan fades, when they stay out of the sun for a while.

Why do redheads get freckles more often than other people?

Redheads don't seem to be able to make enough melanin to get a real tan when they stay in the sun. They only seem to be able to make enough melanin to form those little spots of tan called freckles.

What is frostbite?

Extreme cold can damage body cells just as extreme heat can. Frostbite is an injury to your body's cells caused by too much cold.

What parts of the body are most likely to get frostbitten?

Frostbite is most likely to hit the ears, nose, hands, and feet.

Why are those parts of the body most likely to suffer frostbite?

All those parts are at the extreme ends of some part of the body. There is less blood flowing in those parts. In extreme cold, the body chooses to keep its warmth in the central area where the most important parts are. The outermost parts are the first to get cold.

How do you know if you have frostbite?

Usually the part of your body with frostbite becomes numb. Its color changes to an unnatural white. After the numbness comes a funny, tingling feeling. This is usually followed by real pain.

What is the best thing to do if you think you have frostbite?

Warm the frostbitten part of the body gradually under blankets or in warm, not hot, water. Never try to rub a frostbitten part with snow; that can only make things worse. The best thing of all, however, is to prevent frostbite in the first place, by dressing warmly and keeping your hands and face protected in very cold weather.

11 Sticks and Stones and Broken Bones: Breaks and Sprains

What is a sprain?

Your bones are held together at the joints by a tough sort of material called a ligament. When you take a bad fall or have an accident you may stretch or tear that tough ligament, without actually injuring the bones themselves. That kind of injury is called a sprain.

What happens when you get a sprain?

Your body reacts to the injured cells of the ligament in the same way it does to other injuries— inflammation! More blood rushes to the spot and more fluid is leaked out around the injury. This leads to redness and swelling around the injury. The swelling pushes against pain nerves in the area and causes you to feel pain. The pain is worst when you try to move the bones around the injured ligament.

Why do you feel pain when you get a sprain?

The pain keeps you from moving the injured part very much. The ligament needs to be kept quite still while it is healing. The pain reminds you not to move it!

How do you fix a sprain?

The ligament will repair itself and be as good as new if you don't move it while it is healing. Pain is your body's natural way of keeping you from moving the injured part. But taping up the sprain with an elastic bandage is usually the safest way to keep you from moving a torn ligament while it heals.

What parts of the body are most likely to get sprains?

Ankles and wrists are the most likely parts of the body to get sprains.

How can you tell whether you have a sprain or a broken bone?

Sometimes it's hard to tell if an injury is a sprain or if a bone is broken. In both cases you feel a lot of pain and you have swelling and redness around the injury. The best way to find out whether you have a sprain or a broken bone is to have an X-ray taken. A broken bone will show up clearly on an X-ray.

What is an X-ray and how does it work?

An X-ray is a special kind of invisible wave that can go right through the human body. When the X-ray waves pass through the body they can make shadows of different kinds that can then be seen on a screen or on special film. Different parts of the body cast different shadows, depending on how much of the X-ray wave they can take in. A trained doctor learns to recognize what these shadows look like when everything is normal in the body. Then, when something is wrong, like a broken bone, he can look at the X-ray picture and see clearly that something is very different now.

What happens when you break a bone?

A bad fall or an accident can cause any of your bones to break. Your body reacts to the injury in the same way as it does to a sprain, or any other injury — inflammation. The area around the broken bone becomes red and swollen and very, very painful.

How does a broken bone heal?

Your bones are made of living cells just like your skin, your lungs, your blood, and every other part of your body (except your hair and your nails). Like other cells of your body, bone cells live and die and are able to make new cells just like themselves. When you break a bone, blood soon forms a clot around the two broken ends of the bone. This blood clot forms a base for the bone cells to start making new bone. The bone cells rapidly start making a thick, bony swelling between the two broken ends. As soon as the swelling is thick enough to repair the break entirely the body stops making new bone cells.

Can a broken bone heal by itself?

Yes, bones will heal by themselves. The repair cells will make new bone and knit together a broken bone without any help from a doctor. But unless the bone is set in exactly the same position it was before, and then kept that way without moving while the bone heals, the bone may not heal in the right way. You may end up with a crooked arm, or with one leg shorter than the other.

How can you get the bone in exactly the right position and keep from moving it while it heals?

The doctor can find the exact right position to set the broken bone with the help of X-rays. X-rays will show him when the two ends of the broken bone are meeting exactly right. Then, to keep the bones from moving from that exact position, the doctor will put a plaster cast around the broken bones. This stiff, hard material will keep the ends of the broken bone together and it will keep you from moving them at all, even in your sleep. When the bone has healed, the doctor will take the cast off.

How long does it take for a broken bone to heal?

It depends on the size of the bone and the kind of injury. A small, simple break may heal in less than a month. A badly broken bone may take a year to heal completely.

When a broken bone has healed, is it weaker than it was before?

No, a healed broken bone is at least as strong as it was before it was broken. The bone cells that repair the break grow into a thick layer of new bone called a *callus*. This new bone material is as thick and as strong as the original bone.

12

I'm Allergic! Allergies

What is an allergy?

An allergy is an unusual reaction of the body to something—some food, plant, material, something in the air, medicine, almost anything. If a flame touches your skin you will have a reaction: your skin will get red and a blister will form. But this is not an unusual reaction. This happens to *everyone* when too much heat is put on their skin. This is not an allergy. But if your skin turns red when you eat a certain food while your friends can eat that food without any reaction at all, then you have an allergy to that food.

What happens when you have an allergy?

When you have any sickness caused by germs, your body develops special chemicals called antibodies against the particular germs that are causing the sickness. Then when those germs try to grow in the body again, the antibodies are ready and waiting to attack and kill them.

When you have an allergy your body makes special

antibodies, too, but not against germs. This time your body makes antibodies against some common things that are not usually harmful as germs are—things like dust or cat hairs or different foods. These antibodies then cause trouble every time you come near the thing you are allergic to.

How does an allergy develop?

When you are allergic to a particular thing, your body will make antibodies against that thing the first time you come across it. That first time you will have no bad reaction. If you are allergic to cat hairs, for instance, your body will make anticat antibodies the first time you come near a cat. Then, the *next* time you come near a cat those antibodies will be ready and waiting. This time they will have a *reaction* against the cat hairs. This reaction will cause your body to let out a strong chemical called *histamine* (hís-ta-meen). It is the histamine that causes many of the unpleasant symptoms you feel when you have an allergy.

How does histamine cause the unpleasant symptoms of an allergy?

Histamine is found in certain cells of your body. It is perfectly harmless when it stays inside the cell. When it is let out, however, it somehow causes the body to react in the same way it reacts against germs and injuries—

inflammation! This causes swelling to happen. Thus, in some allergies the histamine makes the nose swell and get runny and the eyes swell and get red.

Why do some people have allergies and others don't?

Nobody really knows why people get allergies. But children whose parents have allergies are more likely to have allergies than children with no allergies in their families. This makes it seem likely that something about allergies is passed on from parents to children.

Do children usually get the same allergies their parents had?

No, children don't always get their parents' allergies. But they will probably be allergic to *something*. They have inherited the tendency to be allergic, not one special kind of allergy.

Are allergies very common?

Yes. About one person out of ten probably has an allergy to something! But there are some things that almost everyone is allergic to.

What is something almost everyone is allergic to?

The answer may surprise you. It is poison ivy! Most people don't know that the rash you get from touching poison ivy is an allergy! But it is. Not everyone gets a rash from touching poison ivy. But *almost* everyone does— about three out of four people are allergic to poison ivy.

What is there about poison ivy that makes people allergic to it?

The three-leaf poison ivy plant has an oily stuff on every part of it, on the leaves, the flowers, the roots and berries. The name of this oily stuff is *urushiol* (oo-róo-shee-ole). It is the urushiol that most people are allergic to.

Can you get a reaction to poison ivy just by getting near to the plant, without actually touching any part of it?

Usually you cannot. You have to touch the plant to get the urushiol on the skin. Only when the urushiol gets on the skin does your body start a reaction against it. But there *is* one way you can get a reaction to poison ivy without touching it. If somebody burns any part of the poison ivy plant in a fire, the urushiol will turn into smoke and travel through the air. Then it can give you a very bad case of posion ivy without your having actually touched the plant.

What are some other things people are allergic to besides poison ivy?

There are a great many things that can cause an allergy in *somebody*. But some things are more likely to cause allergies than others. Some of the common things people are allergic to are: foods—milk, eggs, wheat, chocolates, nuts, strawberries, fish; things in the air you breathe—pollens (tiny parts of plants), dust, animal hairs, cigarette smoke; things you touch—poison ivy, poison oak, poison sumac, wool, furs, leather, plastics, metals, make-up, insect repellents; medicines and drugs, aspirin, penicillin.

How can you find out what you are allergic to?

Some allergies are very obvious. If your face swells up and your eyes start running as soon as you come near a cat, you don't need a doctor to tell you that you're allergic to cats. But usually it's much harder to find out which of the many things you eat, or what things in the air you might be allergic to. Doctors can give you special tests to see if you are allergic to some substances. Doctors can also put you on special diets in which you eat very few different foods and then gradually add new foods one by one. This way they may find what food is causing your allergy.

What are some of the reactions you can have if you are allergic to something?

One reaction, as you have seen, is a rash as in poison ivy. Other reactions are: itching of the skin; swelling up of some part of the body; wheezing and difficulty in breathing air *out* of the lungs; sneezing and a runny nose; runny eyes; headaches; and quite a few other unpleasant symptoms.

Are allergies catching?

Absolutely not!

Can you ever get rid of an allergy once you have it?

One way to avoid trouble from allergies is to keep away from the thing you are allergic to. If you are allergic to strawberries and you never eat strawberries, you won't have any symptoms from your allergy. But you haven't gotten rid of your allergy—you've just gotten rid of the trouble from the allergy.

You can avoid strawberries, or even cats, if those are your allergies. But if you're allergic to something like dust or tree pollens or other things that are everywhere in the air, then it's very hard to keep away from the things that cause you trouble. Then you can get allergy shots from your doctor or from an allergist (a special allergy doctor) that will make your allergy less annoying.

How do allergy shots work?

The doctor gives you an injection under your skin of a very small amount of the very thing you're allergic to. Then after a number of days he'll give you another, slightly larger amount of the substance. As the dose of the injections gets larger and larger, your body begins somehow to get hardened against the allergy. Your symptoms become less troublesome.

Are there any medicines that make allergies better?

There are a number of medicines that help make the symptoms of allergies less unpleasant. The most common medicine for allergy sufferers is *antihistamine* (ant-ee-híst-a-meen). This is a drug that works against that special chemical histamine that causes so much of the trouble for people with allergies. It keeps the histamine from causing as much trouble.

SOME COMMON ALLERGIES

What is hay fever?

Hay fever is an allergy to certain pollens and molds.

What are pollens and how do they cause hay fever?

Pollens are microscopic (too small to be seen without a microscope), yellowish little specks that float around in the air. They come from flowers just about to flower. If you are allergic, when you first breathe in pollens, your body begins to make antibodies against them. Then the next time you breathe in the pollens, the antibodies will cause the symptoms you feel when you have hay fever.

What pollens cause the most trouble for allergic people?

The pollen of a very common American plant called ragweed is one of the greatest causes of allergies. Pine pollens and timothy and other grass pollens are also common offenders.

What are molds and how do they cause hay fever?

Molds are growths that are made up of tiny parts called spores. These mold spores are even smaller than pollen and travel through the air wherever you find molds growing. These spores cause hay fever in the same way pollens do: your body makes antibodies against them. Then every time you come to a place where you breathe in mold spores, the antibodies will start a reaction and you will have hay fever.

What happens when you have hay fever?

The usual symptoms of hay fever are: a runny, stuffy nose; runny, red and itchy eyes; sneezing; stopped–up ears. Some people with hay fever lose their sense of smell for a while.

Why do you sometimes have bad hay fever one day and feel fine the next, even when you're staying in the same place?

The weather has a lot to do with how bad your hay fever will be. On a sunny, dry, windless day during the pollen season there will be a lot of pollen floating around in the air. Your hay fever will be bad. On a rainy day, on the other hand, the rain will bring all the pollen down and you will breathe in hardly any at all. You will not be bothered by hay fever on such a day.

When is the pollen season?

Spring and fall are the worst times, when the most troublesome plants are putting out great quantities of pollen.

Can you catch hay fever from somebody else?

No. Like other allergies, hay fever is not catching.

Is there any way to make hay fever better when you have it?

Yes. You can take allergy shots that help build your body up against the allergy to pollens and molds. You can take antihistamines to help keep down the symptoms of hay fever.

Can you ever be cured of hay fever?

No, you will probably always be allergic to pollens and molds. But you can avoid any trouble from hay fever by keeping away from pollens and molds as much as you can. There are certain parts of the world that are practically pollen-free. Some people move to those places because they don't have to suffer from their allergies there.

What are some places with little or no harmful pollens?

Certain parts of the Catskill and Adirondack mountains are famous for having very few pollens. Oregon and Washington on the west coast have low pollen counts. And there is no ragweed at all in Great Britain and all of Europe.

Is hay fever the only sickness you can get from an allergy to pollens and molds?

No. Another sickness often caused by an allergy to pollens and molds is asthma.

What is asthma?

Asthma is an allergic reaction that causes you to cough and wheeze and have trouble with breathing, especially with the *breathing out* part of breathing.

What are some common causes of asthma?

People with asthma are often allergic to pollens, molds, house dust, and certain animal hairs. Some medicines, drugs, and foods can also bring on asthma.

What happens when you have asthma?

The lining of the air passageways to the lungs swells up. This narrows the space for the air to get in and out of the lungs. The wheezing that usually goes along with asthma is the whistling of air being forced out of the narrowed air passageway.

Is there a way to make asthma better?

There are a number of medicines that can make the symptoms of asthma less unpleasant and that can help people with asthma breathe more easily. There are some very new medicines that seem to help people with asthma avoid getting any symptoms at all, as long as they take those medicines every day. Allergy shots often help people with asthma have less trouble from their allergies. And, as with all allergies, finding out what your allergies are and trying to stay away from those things is the best treatment for asthma.

What is eczema?

Eczema (egg-ze-muh) is a skin condition that is usually caused by an allergy to some food, or to pollens and molds. It is most common among young children.

What happens when you have eczema?

Certain parts of your body become red and rough. Sometimes blisters and a crusty surface appear, with some oozing from the skin. The skin feels terribly itchy when you have eczema, and it is very hard not to scratch it.

What foods most commonly cause eczema?

Milk, wheat, and eggs are very common causes of eczema.

How do you treat eczema?

The first thing to do is to find out what is causing the allergy and to try to stay away from that food or substance.

There are also some ointments and medicines to put on the skin to help it feel better.

What are hives?

Hives are red, puffy swellings on the skin that are caused by an allergy to something, usually a food or a medicine. Hives are very itchy.

What foods and medicines commonly cause hives?

Fish and other seafoods, very spicy foods, strawberries, aspirin, and penicillin are some of the common causes of hives.

How do you treat hives?

As with eczema, the best treatment for hives is to find out what is causing the hives and then to stay away from that thing. Certain ointments will help hives feel less itchy. And some medicines, especially antihistamines, will help the swelling of hives go down.

PART TWO

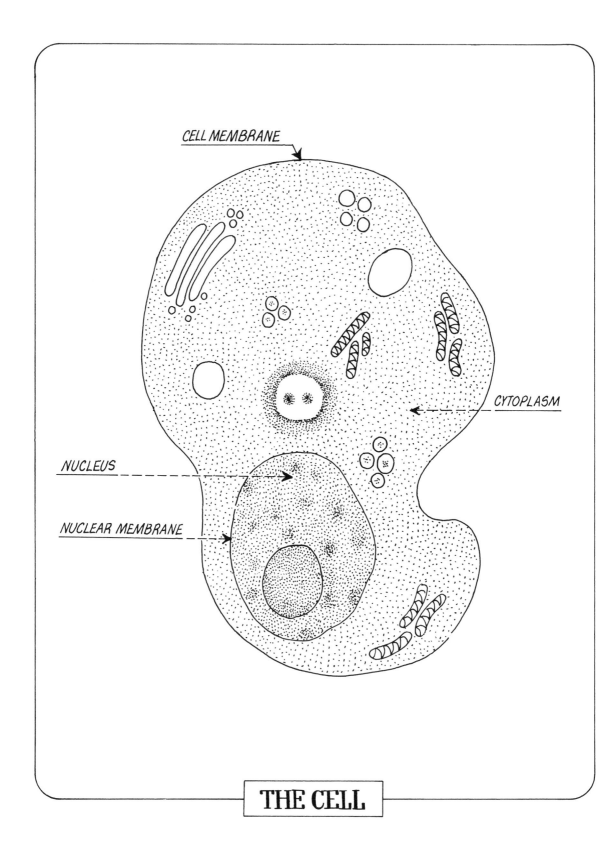

CELL MEMBRANE

CYTOPLASM

NUCLEUS

NUCLEAR MEMBRANE

THE CELL

13 How It Works

HOW IT WORKS: THE CELL

What is a cell?

A cell is the basic unit of life. All living things are made up of cells. Some plants and animals are made up of only one cell. This cell does all the jobs to keep life going. The human body is made of over a trillion cells. These cells do many different jobs to keep the body working. But all the different cells in the body are alike in some ways. They are made of the same materials and contain the same parts.

How big are the cells in your body?

Most cells are so small they can only be seen under a microscope. It takes more than a million cells to make up one square inch of your skin!

What are cells made of?

Inside the cell is a grainy, jellylike fluid. This is the *cytoplasm* (sigh-toe-plasm). It contains many tiny parts that do many of the important jobs of the cell, such as taking in food, making energy, and giving off wastes. In the center of the cell is the *nucleus* (nōo-klee-us). It directs all the work of the cell. The nucleus is a sort of mastermind for the cell, controlling everything that happens. Every cell is surrounded by a thin material called the *cell membrane*. This allows certain materials to pass in and out of the cell.

What do cells do in the body?

Cells are alive. They take in food and use it to make energy. They can multiply and create new cells of their own kind. And in time cells die. Different kinds of cells in the body do different jobs.

What are some of the different kinds of cells in the body and what are their jobs?

Muscle cells	Make your body move.
Nerve cells	Send messages back and forth from the brain.
Blood cells	Red cells carry oxygen to other cells and white cells fight infections.
Bone cells	Build new bones and repair broken bones.
Gland cells	Make chemicals that your body needs.

How do cells change food into energy?

Cells "burn" food to produce energy, but not with hot flames like a fire. Cells manage to change food into energy at the normal temperature of the body, about ninety-eight degrees. It is a very complicated process. Here is an idea how it works:

1. The digestive system breaks down the food you eat into a very simple substance. This can manage to travel through the bloodstream to the cells. The simple substance can enter the cells through the cell membrane.

2. When you breathe you take in a gas called oxygen. Oxygen is carried by the blood to all the cells of your body.

3. When the food and the oxygen meet inside the cell several *chemical reactions* take place. In each of these reactions the food combines with the oxygen somehow. This combining with oxygen is the "burning" of the food. This "burning" makes energy just like a burning fire makes energy. (Put popcorn over a flame and see how a fire makes energy. First the popcorn is completely still. Then it starts to move around in the pan. That moving around is energy, made by the heat of the flame. Just so, the "burning" of your food in your body makes energy that makes you able to move around.) The energy made by the cells then allows the different cells to do their work: a muscle cell tightens and relaxes; a nerve cell sends messages; a gland cell makes special chemicals—and all the other cells have their own special jobs.

How do cells create new cells
of their own kind?

New cells are formed by dividing, so that there are two cells where there once was one. When the cell divides, it splits into two separate daughter cells. Then each daughter cell doubles in size and becomes capable of dividing into two more cells. When the cell divides, most of the activity takes place in the nucleus. Most cells grow and divide over and over again.

What happens when cells die?

Like all living things, cells do die. As your body makes new cells at the rate of about 3 billion every minute, three billion old cells die during the same time period. The dead cells flake off and pass out of the body along with other waste products. Some cells live longer than others. White blood cells live about 13 days before they are replaced. Liver cells live about four months. Only nerve cells live your whole lifetime, which is a lucky thing, since they alone cannot replace themselves if they are destroyed.

HOW IT WORKS: DIGESTION

What is digestion?

Your body needs food to make the energy that keeps all its parts moving. It also needs food to make new cells of all kinds. But your body cannot use the food you eat the way it is when you pop it into your mouth. It is too big. It couldn't get into the cells where it is needed. The food first has to be changed into a very simple liquid before it can be used by all parts of your body. This changing of the food you eat into a simpler form is called *digestion.*

Where does digestion take place in the body?

Digestion takes place in the food canal. This is made up of the mouth, the esophagus (ee-sóf-a-gus), the small intestine and the large intestine. The food canal ends at the rectum, out of which the waste materials of digestion come out when you have a bowel movement.

How does digestion work in the mouth?

The first step of digestion takes place when you chew your food. This breaks it up into smaller pieces. As

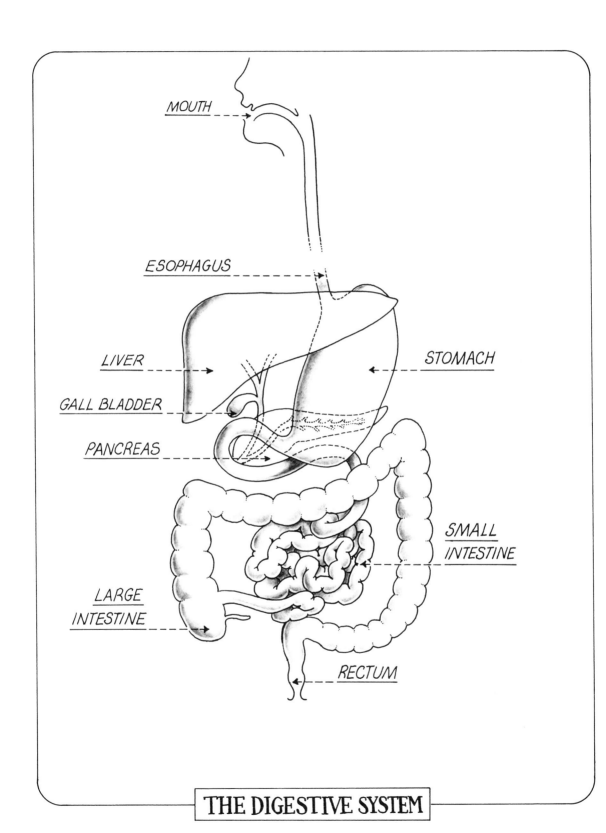

MOUTH

ESOPHAGUS

LIVER

STOMACH

GALL BLADDER

PANCREAS

SMALL
INTESTINE

LARGE
INTESTINE

RECTUM

THE DIGESTIVE SYSTEM

the food is chewed, it gets mixed up with *saliva* (sa-l$\widehat{y}$e-va) in your mouth. The saliva contains some chemicals that help break down the food. By the time you finish chewing your food, it is usually a soft, mushy mixture. Then you swallow it and the food moves down the esophagus on to the stomach, where the next step of digestion takes place.

What happens to the food in the stomach?

In the stomach the food is churned and shaken around by the stomach muscles, while very strong digestive juices pour into the stomach and break up the food into a simpler form. The food stays in the stomach from one to two hours. By the time it is ready to leave the stomach it is a thick liquid. From the stomach the food goes to the small intestine.

What happens to the food in the small intestine?

The most important part of digestion takes place in the small intestine. There the food is finally broken down into the form that can be used by the body's cells. This job is done by other digestive juices that pour into the small intestine from other parts of the body. When the food is completely digested it goes into tiny, threadlike tubes in the walls of the small intestine. From these the food goes directly into the *bloodstream*. The blood then carries the digested food to all parts of the body. Now cells in every part of the body can use the food to make energy and to make new cells. But some parts of the food you eat cannot be broken down into a simple form and sent into the bloodstream. These parts of food pass on from the small intestine into the large intestine.

What happens to the food in the large intestine?

Even though the food that has gone into the large intestine is not useful to the body, that food contains some water that *can* be used. This water now goes back into the bloodstream through the walls of the large intestine. Now what is left is the final waste product, which comes out of the rectum every day or two as a bowel movement.

HOW IT WORKS: BLOOD AND CIRCULATION

What is blood?

Blood is the most important fluid inside the body. It carries oxygen and food to all the cells of the body. It carries waste products away from the cells. It also has special ways of fighting dangerous germs that manage to get inside the body.

How much blood do you have in your body?

It depends on your size and weight. A grown man weighing about 160 pounds has about five quarts of blood in his body. A child weighing about 80 pounds has only two-and-a-half quarts of blood.

What is blood made of?

Blood is made of liquid parts and solid parts. The liquid parts are called *plasma* (pláz-muh). The plasma is 92 percent water. It also contains many chemicals. There are three different solid parts in the blood: *red blood cells*, *white blood cells*, and *platelets*.

What does the plasma do?

All the other parts of the blood float in the plasma to get where they are going. Plasma contains many chemicals that your body needs to stay healthy. It contains antibodies that help fight infection (see page 43). The substance that makes the blood clot and stops a cut from bleeding is also found in the plasma (see page 23).

What are the red blood cells?

The red blood cells are tiny discs. They are so small that one drop of blood contains more than 250 million of them! Their job is to carry oxygen to the cells in all parts of the body.

How do the red blood cells carry oxygen?

The red blood cells contain a special substance called *hemoglobin* (hée-moe-globe-in). This substance can combine very well with oxygen. When hemoglobin combines with oxygen it turns bright red. This is why blood is always red when you get a cut: the oxygen in the air quickly combines with the hemoglobin. The red blood cells with their load of oxygen move through all the parts of the body. They give off their oxygen to the cells. Then they take on a new load: they take away from the cells the waste product left over from the cells' work. This waste product is a gas called *carbon dioxide*. The carbon dioxide leaves your body when you breathe out.

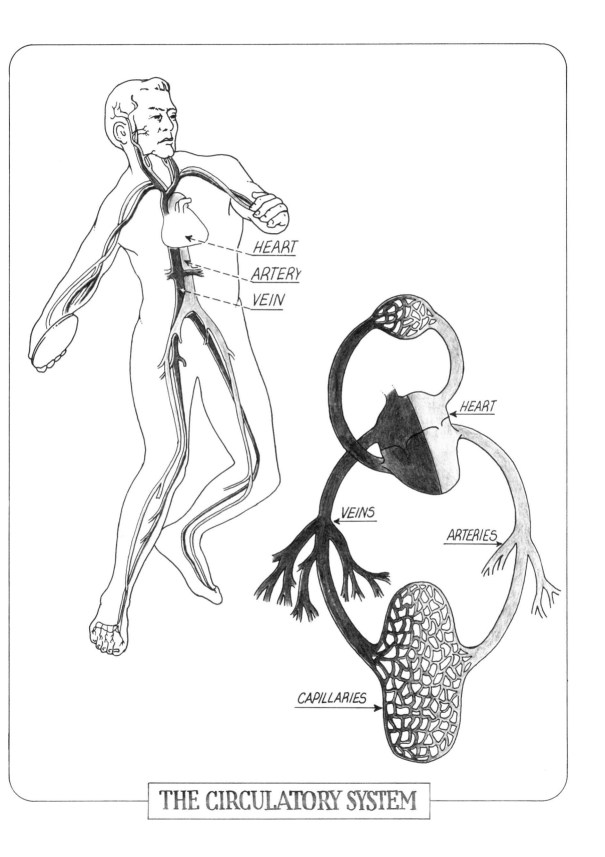

HEART

ARTERY

VEIN

HEART

VEINS

ARTERIES

CAPILLARIES

THE CIRCULATORY SYSTEM

What are the white blood cells?

White blood cells are special cells in the blood that help the body fight against germs. They act as the policemen of the body. When any dangerous germs or poisons from germs enter the body, the white blood cells leave the bloodstream and travel to the area where the danger lies. They can then attack and actually eat up any dangerous germs.

What are platelets?

Platelets are tiny, colorless blobs in the blood. They help repair small blood tubes when there has been an injury. Platelets are also important in helping the blood form a clot, when there has been a cut (see page 23).

What makes the blood go around to all parts of the body?

The heart pumps the blood throughout the body. The heart is actually a muscle that tightens and relaxes about seventy times every minute. Every heartbeat is made up of one tightening and one relaxing of the strong heart muscle. Every heartbeat pumps about two ounces of blood. Since you have more than a hundred thousand heartbeats every day, your heart pumps about thirteen thousand quarts of blood around your body every day.

Does that mean that you have thirteen thousand quarts of blood in your body?

No, you have much less blood than that. But your blood goes around and around, over and over again. That's how your heart ends up pumping thousands of quarts of blood every day, even though you have only a few quarts of blood in your body altogether.

How does the blood actually travel through the body?

The blood travels away from the heart through special elastic tubes called *arteries* (árt-uh-reez). It travels back to the heart in other elastic tubes called *veins* (vanes). In between the arteries and veins are the tiniest blood tubes, called *capillaries* (cáp-ill-eh-reez). The food and oxygen being carried by the blood goes directly to the cells from these tiny capillaries. Then the wastes from the cells go back into the capillaries and then into the bloodstream on their journey out of the body.

Here is how a complete round trip of blood through the body works:

1. The blood is forced from the right side of the heart into an artery that leads to the lungs.
2. In the lungs the red blood cells take on a load of oxygen. They also give up their load of carbon dioxide, one of the waste products of cells.
3. Now the blood with its new load of oxygen leaves the

lungs and goes back to the heart through a vein.

4. Next the blood leaves the heart in another artery and is pumped by the heart throughout the body. It travels into smaller and smaller arteries and finally into the tiny capill-aries throughout the body.

5. Now many things happen. The blood goes through the kidneys and gets rid of more waste products. The blood goes through the intestines and takes on a load of food that has been digested.

6. Throughout the body the blood gives off its load of oxygen and food to the cells, supplying the energy that lets you move, run, and be healthy. Then the blood takes on a load of carbon dioxide from the cells.

7. Now the capillaries lead the blood to the veins. The blood travels along larger and larger veins until it reaches the heart again. It has finished a round trip. It is ready to go to the lungs again to pick up a new load of oxygen.

HOW IT WORKS: BREATHING

What happens when you breathe?

When you breathe *in*, your lungs fill up with air. Oxygen from the air passes from the lungs into your bloodstream. The blood carries the oxygen to all the cells of your body. The blood also carries away carbon dioxide, one of the waste products of your cells, and carries it to the lungs. When you breathe *out*, the carbon dioxide leaves your body through your mouth and nose.

Why do the cells of your body need oxygen?

The cells need oxygen in order to be able to "burn" the food they use for making energy. Without oxygen the cells could not stay alive. When the cells have finished using food and oxygen to make energy, they give off carbon dioxide as a waste product.

How do the lungs work?

The lungs are two spongy baglike things that lie in the chest cavity. The lungs are made up of millions of tiny air sacs. The walls of each of these air sacs are filled with many tiny capillaries. Between your chest and your stom-

ach is a sheet of muscles called the *diaphragm* (dĭ-a-fram).
This goes up and down regularly, pushing air in and out of
your lungs. When the air enters the lungs it is sucked into
the air sacs. From the air sacs the oxygen from the air goes
into the bloodstream as it is passing through the capillaries. The same air sacs receive the carbon dioxide
brought by the blood from the rest of the body cells. Then,
when you breathe out, the carbon dioxide is forced out of
the air sacs and out of the lungs through the mouth and
nose.

How fast do you usually breathe?

A grownup takes about 16 breaths a minute when
awake and about six to eight breaths a minute when
asleep. Children breathe a little more quickly than
grownups.

What makes you breathe faster sometimes?

When you run or exercise, your muscles work hard
and cause large amounts of carbon dioxide to go into the
bloodstream. As the blood goes around and reaches the
brain it goes through a special breathing center. When
blood with extra carbon dioxide reaches the breathing
center, the carbon dioxide acts as a signal: MORE OXY-
GEN NEEDED! LESS CARBON DIOXIDE NEEDED! This
makes the brain send messages to the muscles around the
lungs and to the diaphragm to work harder. This makes
you breathe faster. In this way you take in more oxygen
when your body needs it.

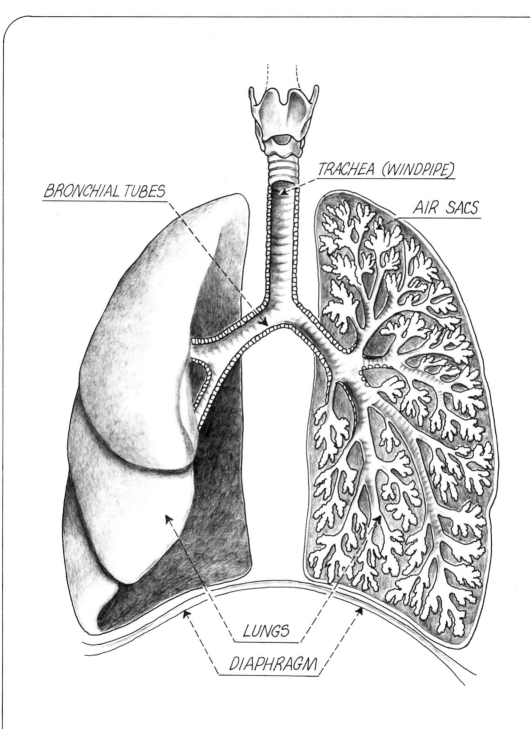

BRONCHIAL TUBES

TRACHEA (WINDPIPE)

AIR SACS

LUNGS

DIAPHRAGM

THE RESPIRATORY SYSTEM

HOW IT WORKS: THE SKIN

What is the skin?

The skin is not merely a covering for other parts of the body. It is an important part of the body itself. It does important work to keep the body healthy. Many important blood tubes, nerve cells, and glands are found in the skin.

What work does the skin do?

The skin does three main jobs:

1. It protects the other parts of the body from injury and keeps germs out of the body.
2. It helps keep the body temperature from getting too high or too low.
3. It is the home of a large number of nerve cells that make it possible to feel things and to sense hot and cold.

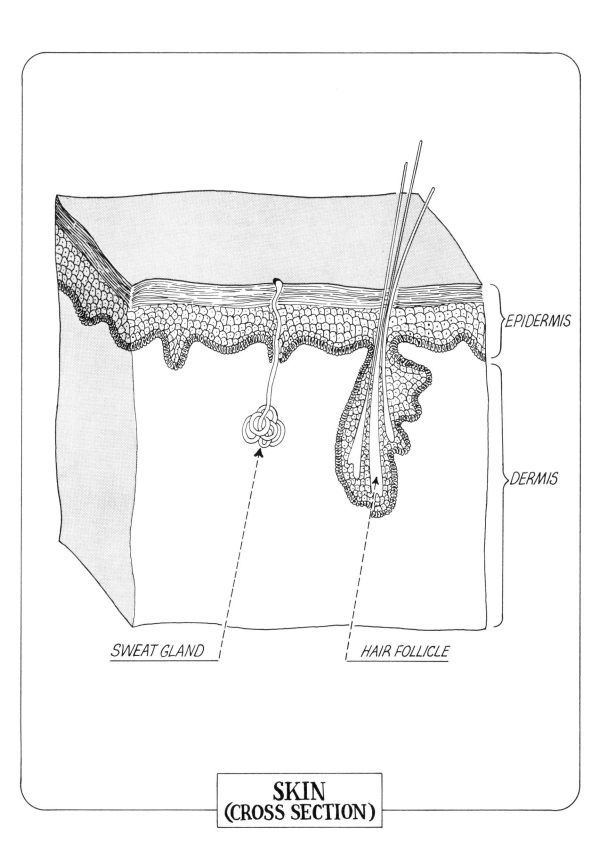

EPIDERMIS

DERMIS

SWEAT GLAND

HAIR FOLLICLE

SKIN
(CROSS SECTION)

How does the skin keep the body temperature from getting too high or low?

If the body is getting too hot and needs to lose some heat, the tiny blood tubes in the skin stretch and grow larger, thus placing the blood closer to the outside air. When the body is getting too cold the blood tubes in the skin tighten up and get smaller. This helps keep heat in the body. Also, the sweat glands in the skin help keep your body cool if it's getting too hot.

What is skin made of?

Skin is made up of two separate layers. The top layer is called the *epidermis* (eh-pi-dér-miss). It is made up of special cells that are placed side by side in neat rows. There are many layers of these cells. There are no blood tubes in the epidermis.

The lower layer is called the *dermis* (dér-miss). In it are many tiny blood tubes, nerves, and sweat glands. The dermis fits into the epidermis exactly, like two parts of a solid jigsaw puzzle. The dermis is sometimes called "the true skin" because that's where most of the important work of the skin takes place.

What are sweat glands?

Sweat glands are small, coiled-up structures. that are able to produce a special liquid called sweat. There are sweat glands all over your body, working all the time. But when the body gets hot they work harder.

How do sweat glands work to cool the body?

When the body is getting too hot and the tiny blood tubes get larger, this brings more blood to the sweat glands in the lower layer of your skin. This makes the glands work harder and make more sweat. The sweat comes out on the surface of the skin and begins to evaporate as it meets the air. This cools the skin. Try wetting your arm on a hot day. As the water evaporates your arm will feel cooler than the rest of the body.

HOW IT WORKS: BONES AND MUSCLES

What do the bones in the body do?

The bones help hold up the softer parts of the body. They hold the body in a definite shape. If there were no bones the body would be a shapeless, formless blob! The bones also act as protection. If you had no ribs, for instance, any small fall or push might injure the heart or lungs or some other important soft part of the body.

The bones, together with the muscles, are important in letting you move all the parts of your body. Besides supporting the body and protecting its parts from injury, the bones themselves produce red blood cells and store calcium, a very important element for health and especially for growth.

What is a bone made of?

The outside of a bone is made of a hard, dense material. The next layer is a spongy material. The inside of a bone is hollow. In the hollow part is the bone marrow. The marrow of some bones is yellow, and it is mostly a

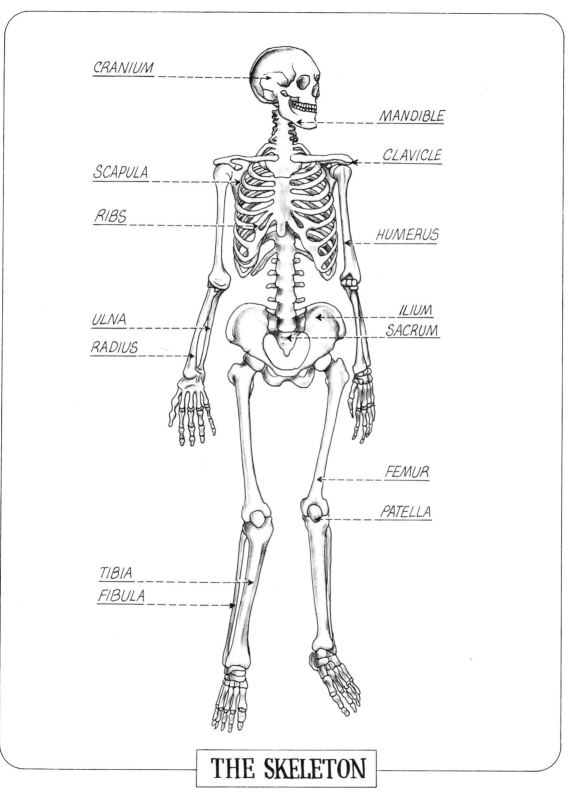

CRANIUM

MANDIBLE

CLAVICLE

SCAPULA

RIBS

HUMERUS

ULNA

ILIUM

SACRUM

RADIUS

FEMUR

PATELLA

TIBIA

FIBULA

THE SKELETON

These are the names of some of the bones.

storage place for extra fat in the body. The marrow of other bones is red, and is made up of blood cells and special cells that make new red and white cells for the body.

How many bones are there in the body?

A baby has many more bones than a grown-up, sometimes as many as 350 bones. But as he grows older, many of those bones grow together to form single bones. Most grown-ups have 206 bones.

How are the bones connected to each other?

The meeting place of two bones is called a *joint.* There are two kinds of joints: movable joints for those bones that move, like the arm and leg bones, and immovable (nonmoving) joints for bones that do not move freely, like those in the skull. The bones that do not move are held together at the joints by a very tough, springy material called *cartilage* (cárt-ill-edge). Holding the movable joints together is a different kind of tough material called *ligament* (líg-uh-ment).

What makes the bones move?

Bones have no way of moving by themselves. They can only move because of the action of the *muscles* (mússels).

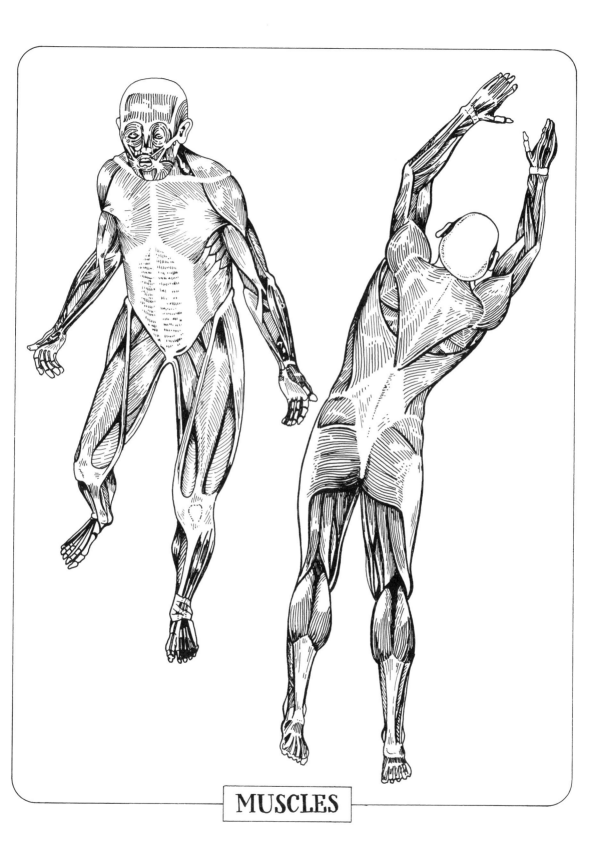

MUSCLES

What are muscles?

Muscles are collections of a special kind of cell that allows all movement in the body to take place. There are three kinds of muscles in the body: smooth muscles, which are found in the walls of veins and arteries (it is these muscles that allow the veins and arteries to get bigger or smaller when necessary), and also in the stomach, intestines and other soft parts of the body; heart muscles which allow the heart to do its work; and skeleton muscles which are attached to all your bones and allow the bones to move.

How do muscles manage to move?

Muscles are made out of special cells that have a special ability: they can tighten up and relax. When a muscle tightens up, it pulls on the bone to which it is attached. This makes the bone move.

How many muscles are there in the body?

The body has more than six hundred muscles. More than half of the body's weight is made up of muscles.

How are muscles connected to bones?

The muscle is attached to the bone by means of a tough cord called a *tendon* (tén-done).

HOW IT WORKS: NERVES

What is a nerve?

A nerve is a special kind of cell that can send messages from the brain to different parts of the body, and messages from parts of the body back to the brain.

What kind of messages do nerves send?

Certain nerve cells can send messages about heat and cold, light and darkness, sounds, smells, and tastes. Other nerves send messages that cause the heart to beat faster, cause blood tubes to open wider or become narrower, and other changes to happen in the body. Inside the brain, nerves send messages to each other. That is how you *think*.

How big is a nerve cell?

Nerve cells vary in size. Some are very short while others can go all the way from your head to the base of your spine, or from your spine to the tip of your toes!

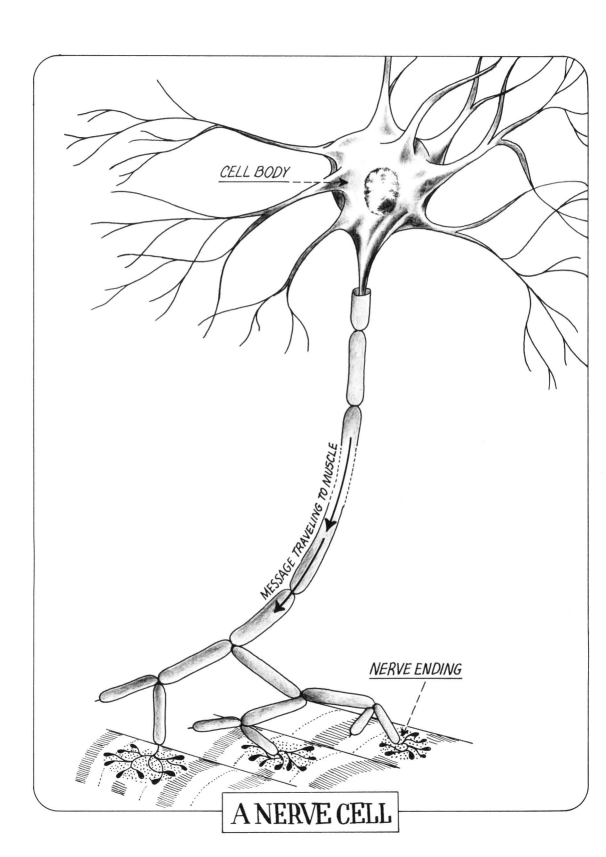

CELL BODY

MESSAGE TRAVELING TO MUSCLE

NERVE ENDING

A NERVE CELL

How do nerve cells send messages
to the brain and back?

A nerve cell is specially designed for the purpose of sending messages. It is made of a small cell body and a very long, thin tail. The tail of one nerve cell is in touch with the head of another. Messages pass along from one nerve cell to the next. In this way a message can travel from your foot to your head in less than a single second.

What *is* the message that is sent
along the nerve cells?

The message is actually made of electricity. Nerve cells are specially made so that they can carry a small amount of electricity. This bit of electricity is what tells your muscles to move and what makes you see, hear, smell, touch, and do all the other things you do.

Where are the nerves in your body?

Nerves spread everywhere in the body like a great network of telephone wires. In some places there are thousands of nerves clustered together. One such place is the *spinal cord* inside your backbone. This is like a great cable containing thousands of nerves lying side by side, leading to the brain.

PART THREE

14

A Few More Words about Being Sick

Now you know some interesting things about runny noses, coughs and sneezes, aches and pains, and all sorts of sicknesses. You probably know more about these things than your friends. You may even know more than your parents and many grownups. Just for fun, try asking your parents or your teacher why you shiver when you have a fever, or why you get a bump from a mosquito bite, or some other question in this book. You will seem very smart to be able to explain these things to your parents and friends. Here are some other ways to seem very smart:

FANCY NAMES

Doctors often use fancy names for some of the ordinary sicknesses and symptoms people have. Here is a list of some of them. Try using the fancy names instead of the ordinary ones with your parents or friends. They'll think you're a genius!

The Common Name—The Doctors' Fancy Name

a runny nose—rhinitis (rye-nye-tiss)

a stomachache—gastritis (gas-try-tiss)

an earache—otitis media (oh-tie-tiss meed-ee-a)

a nosebleed—epistaxis (ep-iss-tax-iss)

a sore throat—pharyngitis (fa-rin-jíe-tiss)
a hoarse voice—laryngitis (la-rin-jíe-tiss)
hiccups—singultus (síng-gul-tuss)
diarrhea—enteritis (en-ter-rýe-tiss)
a fever—pyrexia (pie-réx-ee-a)
overweight—obesity (oh-beé-si-tee)
paleness—pallor (pál-ler)
a jagged cut—laceration (la-sir-á-shun)
a mole—nevus (neé-vus)
an injury—trauma (trów-ma)
warts—verruca (ver-oó-ka)
dizziness—vertigo (vér-tih-go)
hives—urticaria (er-tick-ár-ee-a)
bleeding—hemorrhage (hém-or-idge)
swelling—edema (ed-eé-ma)
vomiting—emesis (em-eé-sis)
redness of skin—erythema (er-ith-eé-ma)
a bruise—contusion (con-toó-zhun)
itching—pruritus (proo-rýe-tis)

ENDINGS

Many of the endings of medical words have a
meaning that help explain what the whole word means.
Here are the meanings of some of the common medical
endings.

The ending *-itis* always means an inflammation. So if
you hear the word *tonsillitis*, you can figure out that it
means an inflammation of the tonsils.

The ending *-ectomy* always means that something is

being cut out or removed. It usually describes an operation. Therefore, if you hear the word *appendectomy*, you can figure out that it means an operation where the appendix is removed.

DOCTORS' NAMES

There are three kinds of medical doctors. Some care for patients with all kinds of sicknesses and troubles. These are called *general practitioners* or *G.P.'s* or *family doctors.* Some specialize in certain kinds of sicknesses or treatments. These are called *specialists.* And some work at learning more about the body and how it works, trying to find new ways of dealing with sickness. These doctors are called *researchers.*

Most specialists have fancy names that describe their special field. You might want to know some of these names:

A pediatrician specializes in children's sicknesses.
A dermatologist deals with skin problems.
An allergist deals with allergies.
A cardiologist specializes in heart problems.
An ophthalmologist is an eye specialist.
An orthopedist specializes in bones, joints, and ligaments.
A surgeon does different sorts of operations.
A radiologist is an X-ray specialist.
An anaesthesiologist specializes in putting people to sleep before they have an operation.
Psychiatrists and neurologists deal with problems of the mind and the nervous system.

An otolaryngologist (also called an E.N.T. doctor) deals with ear, nose, and throat problems.

WHEN YOU HAVE TO TAKE SOME MEDICINE...

When the doctor decides that you need some medicine to help you get better he usually writes out a *prescription* (pree-skrip-shun). A prescription is a written order from the doctor to the druggist for certain medicines that can only be sold if a doctor orders them. The prescription also tells how much medicine to take and how many times a day you need to take it. To save time, doctors use a special code to write the instructions about taking medicine on the prescription. Then the druggist writes the instructions on the medicine bottle label in words that you can understand. But it's fun to be able to read a doctor's prescription. Here are some of the prescription code words and what they mean:

q.h. means every hour

a.c. means before meals

p.r.n. means whenever necessary

b.i.d. means twice a day

t.i.d. means three times a day

q.i.d. means four times a day

tsp. means teaspoon

tbs. means tablespoon

So, if the prescription says 1 tsp. t.i.d., you know that you have to take one teaspoon of medicine three times a day. Usually you have to keep taking the medicine until the bottle is empty.

PARTS OF THE BODY

Doctors sometimes use fancy words to refer to common parts of the body. Here are some of them:

a digit is a finger or a toe
hallux is the big toe
gingiva are the gums around the teeth
glossa is the tongue
umbilicus is the navel or belly button
tympanic membrane is the ear drum
integument is the skin
extremities are the arms or legs

OTHER FANCY WORDS DOCTORS USE

Sometimes doctors seem to be speaking in a foreign language when they use special medical terms. Here, just for fun, are some sentences written in "doctorese" and then translated into ordinary English:

You've had a serious *trauma* to the *integument* of your left *hallux*. Please remain *recumbent* and do not remove the *dressing* until the *edema* disappears.

(You've had a bad *injury* to the *skin* of your left *big toe*. Please remain *lying down* and don't take off the *bandage* until the *swelling* goes away.)

During your *convalescence*, please do not *ingest* any vegetables and please *masticate* well when you eat to prevent *emesis* from recurring.

(While you are *getting better*, please don't *eat* any vegetables and please *chew* your food well when you eat so that you don't *throw up* again.)

That mushroom you ate was *toxic*. It is causing *torpor, pallor,* and *somnolence*. I will give you a *palliative*, but you will suffer from *vertigo* for a few hours.

(You ate a poisonous mushroom. It's making you *sluggish, pale,* and *sleepy.* I will give you a *medicine that will make you feel better,* but you will still be *dizzy* for a few hours.)

Index
